PTSD
& A Drug-Free Me

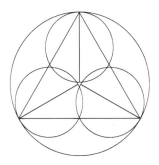

Get Real about Handling Trauma without
Abusing Drugs, Alcohol, or Prescription Meds

CATHERINE SCHERWENKA

PTSD and a Drug-Free Me
Get Real about Handling Trauma without Abusing Drugs,
Alcohol, or Prescription Meds

Difference Press, Washington, D.C., USA
Copyright © Catherine Scherwenka 2019

ISBN 978-1-68309-244-5

Cover Design: Jennifer Stimson
Editor: Cory Hott
Author's photo courtesy of: Kristina Muller
Logo Design: Kristina Muller

DP
DIFFERENCE
PRESS

ADVANCE PRAISE

PTSD and a Drug-Free Me is *the* handbook for understanding the mind-body-spirit connection, and how to find and utilize one's own internal strength for healing. Catherine's passion for helping others learn to access the power of mindfulness to find calm in the midst of chaos is genuine and inspiring. Her book brings clarity to the confusion caused by pain and shines a light on the inner peace that is possible for everyone.

~ Terri Keener, LCSW, LSCSW ~

In this inspiring book, Catherine gently guides us through a journey back to our authentic self, a place where transformation is waiting to happen. Her simple, poignant reflections and meditations allow an opening of heart, a growth in awareness, and a shift in consciousness. Catherine skillfully reveals invaluable insights that are creatively woven through the lens of her own life experiences.

~ Dr Maureen Muller Cultural Leader ~

Catherine Scherwenka has written a very important book that provides insights to the origins of post-traumatic stress disorder, its manifestation in daily life, and its impact on interpersonal relationships. She describes a drug-free treatment for PTSD. Drawing on her own personal experience with PTSD and how it impacted her life, she is able to connect with people who are suffering from the same disorder and guide them through a process that helps them to gain insight into what is happening to their once "normal" life.

~ Larry Harikian, MD ~

I have been a prosecutor for eighteen years, handling cases of child abuse and neglect, child homicides, and child sexual abuse… I took pride in being the best compartmentalizer. I could avoid emotions at all cost. As I got older I realized the years of numbing the bad feelings also impacted the good feelings which was impacting my relationships. *PTSD and a Drug-Free Me* is so personal, as if the author was in your living room. Her words made me feel safe to start feeling again, no matter how frightful that journey can be. Her personal narrative, as well as the stories of others, made me feel connected to a community where I would not be seen as weak or "crazy." The step-by-step tactics to move toward awareness and becoming connected again empowered me to be ready to take on the next path of my life as me.

~ B. Duffy, Chief Deputy District Attorney,
Juvenile Division ~

This book is a must-read for anyone who is having a difficult time handling a traumatic incident they've gone through. After going through the trauma of the 1 October shooting in Las Vegas, I was experiencing a level of stress that I've never felt before. I truly believe Catherine and her techniques were the one thing that assisted me to start managing the stress I was feeling. Prior to managing the coroner's office through the mass shooting in Las Vegas, I had never tried mediation. Since being introduced to Catherine and learning the techniques she offered, I have made it a priority to practice her techniques multiple time a week. This regular practice has helped me to manage my mental health in ways that are difficult to comprehend. I highly recommend this book and encourage people struggling to follow the steps Catherine provides to minimize the stress they are experiencing.

~ John Fudenberg, D-ABMDI, Coroner of the Clark County Office of the Coroner/Medical Examiner ~

For my mama, Jean Scherwenka,
who had a dream to publish a book,
this one is for YOU!

for my papa, Thomas Scherwenka: if it weren't for you?
Not sure I'd be here today.

Kandy, you've inspired me in more ways
than you'll ever know, thank you.

And Tim, thank you for taking such good
care of our mama.

I love, honor, and respect each one of you.
Thank you.

I've used the term 'PTSD' as the title of my book because it is widely recognizable and still useful as a clinical diagnosis, however I believe that by calling Post Traumatic Stress a 'disorder', it puts an un-necessary stigma on the person which keeps one from feeling that he/she can truly heal. This clinical diagnosis is not a brand we have to wear forever and I feel that dropping the 'D' is a healthy beginning to living a new life.

TABLE OF CONTENTS

FOREWORD

I first met Catherine Scherwenka in the blur of months following the mass shooting in my hometown. Her sheer presence brought me to a pause. I had the opportunity to sit in meditation and experience the healing she is creating space here in Las Vegas.

Months before the 1 October massacre in Las Vegas, I was working at the new UNLV School of Medicine. I serve as the Director of Wellness and Integrative Medicine, where we incorporate wellness and integrative healing practices into our medical curriculum. All of my work had been focused on the medical students, residents, fellows, and faculty – until the morning of October 2, 2017. I woke up to the horrific news and knew that the role was now to serve the community.

This book is the missing link to my own healing journey, and I am certain many others. Catherine's ability to share her own experiences and creation of a six-step process is transformative. I hope you enjoy the journey with this special woman just as I have.

Happy reading and new creation.

Dr. Anne Weisman
Director of Wellness and Integrative Medicine
UNLV School of Medicine

CHAPTER 1
PTSD AND TRAUMA SUCKS, BUT SO DOES TAKING PRESCRIPTION DRUGS!

Lucy

It was the first day of a two-day retreat, and I asked each person in the group to take a moment to reflect, and then share why they had decided to come to the retreat and what they hoped to get out of it.

Lucy went first.

"Hi, my name is Lucy, and I am thirty-two years old. I've been on prescription meds for nine months now and I hate it. My doctor told me he thinks I have PTSD [post-traumatic stress disorder] because of the panic attacks I've been having and the fact that I don't like to run anymore, which used to be my favorite hobby before the shooting. I hate taking the meds because they make me feel numb, completely disconnected from my body, and I feel stuck. But I'm also petrified to stop taking them 'cause my doctor told me I shouldn't stop – he should know best – and because I'm scared I'll fall back into the dread pit of despair where I get gripped in fear wondering if I'll ever be able to feel like I did before the incident that feels like it took my life away. And then another panic attack."

I could feel Lucy's sense of hopelessness, yet I felt a surge of excitement that she had committed to the weekend because I knew she was ripe for transformation and that a profound, internal shift could happen for her.

"One more thing," Lucy said. "You have a deck of cards in the sacred space over there in the middle of the room, and last night when I first arrived, and then again when I came in this morning, even after I shuffled the deck several times, I've pulled the same card twice. It's the 'I am sensitive' card. Can you tell me why?"

I smiled and said, "Thank you for your authentic share, Lucy. I know it's not easy to be vulnerable and to state where we're really at with our trauma. We'll have a lot of time to go deeper into this over the weekend, but in regard to pulling the 'sensitive' card, oftentimes when someone endures any sort of trauma, they become more sensitive to sights, sounds, visions, touch, smells. But most of us aren't taught how to live in the world as a more sensitive person, so it can sometimes feel scary and overwhelming. Perhaps you're being shown that card to help you embrace being more sensitive and to allow for that. This weekend will help you."

Living Inside the Trauma

Here is what generally happens after someone endures a trauma.

The traumatic incident occurs. The affected person appears to have somehow navigated through it, yet after a few weeks or even a few months, her behavior starts to change. She becomes more irritable, anxious, worried, impatient, confused, obsessive, compulsive, or depressed and may even start engaging in self-destructive habits. The next thing you know, she's taking prescription meds (which she's not really into taking because her mom raised her to believe it's best to heal yourself as naturally as possible), she's drinking more booze than she ever has before, and she is feeling such a sense of hopelessness from the fact that she doesn't believe there can be any other way to heal; her life is spiraling downward.

Life is our most unreliable narrator. It is a journey filled with so many roads that lead you up and down and can take you to places you sometimes didn't intend to go. Just when you think you have it all figured out, something inevitably shows up to prove you otherwise, which can often derail you and even become a trauma in your mind, body, and spirit.

Side Note: What do I mean when I reference the body-mind-spirit? Body is physical body: bones, blood, organs, skeleton, and muscles, all of the systems that are in place that give you the experience of being a human being. Mind is your thoughts, thinking, and emotions; it's what allows us to discern and use judgment. I'll be sharing more on this later. And spirit? This I like to refer to as your higher sacred self. Some name it God, Creator, Universe, Light, Nature – whatever you feel a connection to outside of yourself. It's what creates synchronicities, magic, and that feeling of expansion.

After suffering through a trauma, the ways in which you've been taught to deal with stress and anxiety up until that point – maybe to speak positive affirmations or to suck it up and muscle your way through it – suddenly don't seem to work anymore. Instead of heading down the road to recovery, you find yourself slipping into a deep, dark rabbit hole of no return. Everything begins to feel negative where all you perceive is what's wrong with life instead of what's great; your relationships feel dry and unfulfilling, and life seems to be closing in on you.

Why?

Wisdom of an Elder

There is a story of two Buddhist monks walking home after spending a long day at a nearby village helping people in need. One was an elder, while the other was new to the monastic order and quite young. They walked in silence and came to the river's edge where a woman stood and cried.

The elder asked, "Are you okay?"

She responded, "My daughter is only three years old and is waiting for me back at our village, but I need to get across the river, and now it has gotten too high and I am not able to cross."

Without thinking, the elder monk picked the woman up, put the woman over his shoulder, and walked across the river. When they got to the other side, the elder gently put her down, bowed his head, and continued to walk.

After some time, the elder could sense the younger monk was feeling anger and so he finally broke the silence and said, "Do you have something to share with me?"

Immediately, the younger monk spewed out in a sort of disgust, "Our master tells us not to look at a woman, but you spoke to her. Our master tells us not to touch a woman, but you carried her. How could you do this?"

The elder looked at the younger monk and replied, "I left the woman alongside the bank of the river forty-five minutes ago, but you seem to be still carrying her. Why?"

This is the nature of the mind. It is what happens when something triggers in the mind and we are not able to let it go. The mind gets caught in obsessive, self-centric thinking, and we feel trapped. We are not able to control the thoughts, and they eventually wreak havoc on our existence.

But after enduring a trauma, this thinking becomes even more challenging, sometimes almost unbearable, where the mind is constantly chattering, and you start to wonder if you'll ever feel at peace again.

Trauma is a wake-up call. It can be perceived as an obstacle or an opportunity. I like to think of it as an opportunity to stop and take a good look at your life, at the choices you've made, and ask yourself, "Is this the life I really want to be living?" We are so good at building a glass castle around us, making ourselves and our lives look pretty, comfortable, and sweet. And many of us will "get by" fine doing that. But when a traumatic incident occurs, it oftentimes will shatter the glass castle and everything that you built up around it. And what you thought you had once wanted, loved, and believed in, suddenly becomes meaningless, empty, and dry, and you begin to wonder what the meaning of life is.

Are you ready to take back your life and live it the way you intended too without having what happened in your past influence your today? Are you ready to no longer be a victim of circumstance and instead be in your true, innate power? Are you ready to drop the stories from the past that have tainted your today?

How do we do this is the question.

This book is a map that will help you to discover where you are today inside the scope of healing the trauma and PTSD that has taken a piece of your life away. It is an inward journey that will guide you to navigate back to your place of truth, authenticity, self-forgiveness, and self-compassion.

You will find your inner radiance, your inner vitality, and your beautiful inner strength that will propel you forward on the path of truly living. You will feel emotionally stable, grounded in your body and ready for life again.

By not making the conscious choice to say *yes* to *yourself*, you are merely just existing and not really living. Maybe you want to manifest your dream partner, but since the traumatic incident took place, you've not been able to stay in a committed relationship or even find someone of interest. Maybe the job you're at is no longer serving your highest good, is no longer fulfilling, and you're ready for change but you feel scared, gripped by fear and therefore unable to make a move. Perhaps your body has taken a toll since the traumatic incident took place and is silently screaming out for some love, attention, self-care, and affection.

By committing and saying yes, you have just opened up the door of healing. You've released a valve that's been sealed tight, and the air is starting to circulate and move again, allowing your breath to deepen. All of this is happening just because you are saying yes. The hardest part of the recovery process is admitting that there is something wrong. We live in a culture that prides itself on perfectionism and the reality is, there is no such thing.

Making a Commitment

Close your eyes and imagine holding the hands of someone you love dearly, a person you feel the most connection with. This person could be alive or perhaps this person has already passed, but make sure it's someone you feel one hundred percent comfortable with.

It could also be your higher sacred self or God.

Internally say to yourself, I am safe, I am grounded, I am present.

Ask this person (not in real life, but energetically), to hold your hands throughout the process that this book takes you through and to never let go. At any point throughout the book, when you feel like you're shutting down, you want to run away, or you want to give up, remember holding this person's hand and say to yourself, "I'll never let go. Please stay with me, help me to stay strong, help me to shed whatever it is that is keeping me from living the life I know I want to be living."

Express gratitude for this connection you have.

CHAPTER 2
SEPTEMBER 11, 2001

My American Dream

I was a midwestern girl who, at the age of twenty-two, took a leap of faith and moved to Manhattan, New York, to live out my dream. I quickly worked my way up the ladder of beauty, hair, and fashion and opened what came to be an uber-successful business whose clients consisted of celebrities, VIPs, entrepreneurs, and stay-at-home moms with nannies. I somehow managed to create a life that, from the outside looking in, appeared as the American dream. I was engaged to be married to a Wall Street broker who sealed the proposal with a sparkly Tiffany diamond ring, which led me to the perfect silk-and-tulle strapless wedding dress that shimmered with the color of champagne, and when all combined, brought out the queen in me. It was to take place at an Italian-style villa perfectly nestled amid the Napa Valley vineyards where I was prepared to say, "I do" to a man I had thought was going to complete the remainder of my American dream, with marriage, two kids, a dog, and white picket fence. It glimmered with the hope of promise, a promise that I was going to live a happy, healthy, fulfilling life.

I was always a downtown girl, and if you know anything about Manhattan, you'll understand what I mean. I was the more creative type, lived most of my time in Soho, and felt connected to the people and the diversity that is downtown. I felt like no matter what size, shape, color, sexual preference, or religion, you were all right. It's where the more alternative people hung out and that inspired me.

Katrina, my soon-to-be business partner, lived around the corner from me in Soho in her own studio apartment. After we both worked our way up the ladder at Frederic Fekkai and John Barrett Salon, we decided to do the unthinkable and leave our very secure, consistent, high-paying, lucrative jobs to open up our own version of the chic, upscale salon de coiffure, but instead of doing it where everyone else did it – on Fifty-Seventh and Fifth Avenue – we decided we were moving uptown downtown.

We were ready to take a chance.

We did take a chance.

And we hit it.

Within the first few months of our grand opening, we could barely keep up with the revolving door of excited clients ready to experience the "downtown vibe" we were proud to be serving. We served wine and beer during appointments (this was before serving booze with a haircut became trendy), as well as tasty finger foods like cheese and crackers, fresh fruit, olives, and chocolate to delight the palette. People were enjoying the downtown ambiance and our fear of failure quickly morphed into "Where are we going next? We've gotta expand."

Let's grow.

School Begins

It was a beautiful, sunny Tuesday morning, and I was up early to do my daily run. My type A personality lent me that false sense of control we type As tend to have; I would look for something, anything, to help me feel like I was actually in control of my life (not knowing that it's only pain that looks for a way to control things). The one thing I did feel I was in control of and what I felt I was a master at controlling was my body. I was an avid runner, a "Lotte Berk" fiend (now known as the "Bar Method"), and I slipped in some yoga here and there only because I knew it was supposed to somehow keep me healthy (according to my mom).

After getting engaged, I moved uptown to live with my fiancé on Eighty-Eighth and York Street, the upper east side of Manhattan (the only six months in all of my eleven and a half years of living in New York City that I didn't live downtown), and I'll never forget running past all of the parents that morning who were dropping off their kids for school. There was excitement intermixed with fear in everyone's faces. It was fall and school just started, so there were kids who were eagerly saying goodbye to their parents, excited to meet new friends, and then there were the ones who were resisting, crying, not wanting to leave their mom or dad and go to this place called "school." All of it brought a smile onto my face as I witnessed these interactions and wove my way across First, Second, Third, Lexington, Park, and Madison, finally reaching Fifth Avenue, where I caught Central Park.

I had just returned home forty-five minutes later, flipped on The Today Show (another one of my type A daily must-dos), sat on the couch, and taken off my running shoes when my (flip) phone rang.

It was my business partner.

"Hi, Katrina! How are you?"

I could only hear sobbing and panting, but Katrina doesn't sob; she doesn't even cry. She is one of those human beings who seem to have it all together and doesn't emote.

"Are you okay?" I asked.

She gasped, "I just saw a plane fly straight down Fifth Avenue and right into the side of the World Trade Center!"

"No, no, Katrina, that couldn't be," I said shaking my head no with a nervous chuckle in my throat. "I'm watching The Today Show, and there is nothing like that on the TV."

Wow, what ignorance – if it's not on The Today Show, then it must not be happening? Jeez.

"No, yes, yes, I just saw it and it's now burning on the side of the building!"

And then it flashed on the television, the tail end of a huge jet airplane hanging off the side of the World

Trade building, enveloped in smoke, flames, papers flying everywhere, and in a flash, I remembered that my fiancé was at work, exactly one block away from where this inferno took place. He was on the twenty-fifth floor, and I needed to get him out.

"I've gotta go, Katrina. I've gotta call Jack and tell him to get out of there!"

I hung up the phone, hands shaking, barely able to dial Jack's number.

"Hello?" Jack said.

My voice trembled, "Honey, do you know what is happening? A jet plane just flew into the side of the World Trade Center! I think you should leave, Jack. Please will you leave right now?"

I was holding back the hysteria that was quivering on the edge. I felt lightheaded and as if my wheels were starting to fall off. I knew in the pit of my stomach that something was very wrong.

"I think it'll be okay, honey, although I can barely see outside my window. It looks like a ticker-tape parade with papers flying everywhere."

"But please Jack, I'm scared – something is really wrong! Will you please come home?"

As I begged and pleaded, he kept responding with a reassurance that everything was going to be okay, that I should just relax.

And then the second plane hit.

I screamed.

I suddenly became tough, as if something had taken over my body, mind, and voice, and sternly said, "Jack, leave right now. Go downstairs and get on the subway and leave now!"

Jack grabbed his briefcase and made it onto the last subway that got out of downtown Manhattan that day, before the walls came tumbling down.

In Remembrance

Pause. Reflect. Where were you that day? What were you doing?

Deep breath.

Honor all those that were lost in the tragedy that day.

Reality Turned Nightmare

Jack was home from work by 10:30 a.m. on September 11, 2001, and we sat all day long watching what felt surreal, watching it all unravel.

How could this be happening in our country, in the U S of A?

Weren't we protected from this sort of thing?

Didn't this only happen in foreign countries far away, like in the Middle East.

The only terrorism I had ever experienced was during the Cold War.

But this? Of this magnitude? Of this horror?

By 2:00 p.m., we were at the neighborhood bar ordering straight-up martinis, drinking more than our bodies could handle. People packed into the bar and the fear was alive in the air. Everyone in the place, desperately trying to gulp down and smother the growing rage and fire that was burning up inside.

The pain. The feeling of helplessness. The hopelessness.

As we watched over 3,000 people die in the most unthinkable, gruesome manner.

Phone lines were down. Families were not able to connect with loved ones to see if they were safe or all right. My mom finally got through to me that evening, but by then, I was passed out on the couch in a haze, floating somewhere between this physical realm and the vodka realm.

Reality was a real-life nightmare and the most comforting place at this point was the dream world.

Why? For what? All in the name of beliefs? Religion? None of it made sense. How could it?

The city shut down for the next couple of days. Everyone was in a cloudy haze of disorientation, not knowing what was real and what was made up.

My mind frantically tried to make sense of something incomprehensible.

I made it back to work by Friday. The city was somber. The smell unbearable.

Shortly after I arrived, Katrina came and found me to let me know that someone was on the phone waiting for me.

"Hello?"

"Is this Catherine?" she asked.

"Yes, it is. Who's this?"

"My name is Charlotte. I'm Brooke's roommate. Are you sitting down?"

Nobody had ever asked that of me before.

My body started to tremble as I found the cushion.

Brooke was my college roommate in Florence, Italy, where we studied Renaissance landscape, art, and design. I hadn't seen or talked to her for two years, but she had just popped into our salon unexpectedly a week prior to 9/11. Even though she and I only spent four months together, they were an unforgettable four months, and she became the little sister I'd never had.

"Yes, I'm sitting down."

"I'm sorry to have to have to be the one to tell you this, but Brooke was on the 102nd floor on Tuesday and didn't make it out. She shared with me how excited she was that the two of you reunited last week and that you were going to have dinner together. I wanted to let you know that she died on 9/11."

My body was reacting faster than my mind could think.

I felt nauseous, my body was trembling, and there was no saliva left in my mouth.

My mind kept repetitively thinking, "But I just saw Brooke a week ago. How is it that she came to see me one week ago and now she's dead?"

We sobbed.

There were few spoken words after that. Only tears.

I hung up the phone and asked the manager to cancel my day. I couldn't do it. I couldn't face anyone. I felt like I could barely function. I had to get out.

The Aftermath

For weeks, the city was filled with sirens and a relentless mourning. There was a veil of guilt for those who had survived, and a stench I had never smelled before and haven't smelled since. I saw random "missing persons" fliers everywhere, and every so often, Brooke's big, brown eyes stared deep into my soul. There were nonstop funeral processions down Fifth Avenue en route to lay those killed to rest at St. Patrick's Cathedral. The church had never held so many visitors.

The 2,996 killed (including the nineteen hijackers) consisted of fathers, mothers, sisters, brothers, aunties, uncles, cousins, friends, colleagues, firefighters, medics, and first responders of all kind, and there were millions of people in psychological pain.

Of those who died, 2,606 were in the World Trade Center, 265 on the airplanes, 125 at the Pentagon. And over 6,000 people were injured.

Most were civilians, except for the 343 firefighters and seventy-one law enforcement officers who were at the World Trade Center, and the fifty-five military personnel at the Pentagon who lost their lives in the line of duty that day. Thank you for your service, for giving your lives so we could keep ours.

Within two weeks of the horrific incident, I found myself in a psychiatrist's office, a hot mess. I couldn't sleep. I couldn't focus. I felt like I was living inside a sea of chaos, and I couldn't gain my footing. I lost the ground beneath me and I was petrified. I had never felt this before and all I knew was that it didn't feel good.

Before I could finish explaining to the doctor what I was experiencing, he labeled me as having PTSD and gave me a prescription medication called Klonopin, which was supposed to calm down the anxiety and panic attacks I wasn't able to control. I was never a proponent of taking prescription drugs, as my mom always felt they broke down the immune system and would suggest alternative methods in order to heal.

But this was different. I was desperate. I was lost. And instead of getting better, I was seemingly getting worse.

I needed help.

Jack lost twenty-five of his closest friends with whom he attended Columbia Business School, and he was in shock and denial. That was one of the defense mechanisms many of us used to try to navigate through this horror: denial. Jack did a great job at appearing to be okay on the outside, but I could tell he was crumbling and falling apart on the inside. He started acting out, behaving strangely, and it concerned me. I insisted we go see a couple's therapist, which he deplored, but in order to appease me, he said yes.

We tried five different therapists, none of whom were to Jack's liking. Each time we struggled, doing our best to find common ground yet never feeling understood by the other, never feeling heard or listened too, and inevitably, Jack would find a flaw with the therapist and on to the next we'd go. The therapist wasn't good enough, smart enough, asked too many questions, didn't ask enough questions. It didn't matter who we saw or how many degrees he had (we definitely didn't see a "she"), he just wasn't good enough.

Within five months of 9/11, my fairy tale American dream life had officially ended. I called off our wedding, moved back downtown, back into my own apartment, where I desperately searched to find myself again. The Klonopin, although it took the edge off, took everything else off along with it. I couldn't feel anything. I felt numb. I felt disconnected. I felt "fine" — but not really. I was drinking more alcohol than I had ever drunk before. I smoked cigarettes and experimented with some street drugs; all in all, I was a torn-up mess.

I couldn't make sense of anything anymore. I found myself asking questions like, "What is the meaning of life? What is the point? Why are we here?" All of which, we know, can never be answered. I went through the motions of "living life" — going to the gym, going to work, then out for dinner every night, drinking a bottle of wine (or two or three) with co-workers and friends —only to find myself night after night deep inside a dark void of emptiness, loneliness, sadness, fear, anger, resentment, self-judgment, and self-hatred. And despite being in one of the busiest cities in the world, I felt lonelier than I'd ever felt before.

The Middle Fork

My brother and sister-in-law who lived in Montana were five and a half months pregnant right around the same time as 9/11 and, due to unforeseen complications, had to give birth prematurely and lost their firstborn son. They called me up one day and asked if I'd like to go on a white-water rafting trip down the Middle Fork of the Salmon River in Idaho as a sort of healing journey that we'd take together. I had never thought of going on a white-water rafting trip before, but I was feeling desperate and wanted to try anything at that point.

I geared myself up from head to toe at Paragon Sports in Manhattan, packed up my bags, and left for a one-week journey down the Middle Fork. From the moment I landed in Idaho, I felt a presence that I hadn't felt in years.

There was a stillness, a peacefulness; everything felt vibrant and alive, and the feeling was visceral.

On the third day of our trip, I decided to float down the river in a double kayak with another passenger whom I didn't know. If you've ever ridden tandem on a bike or in a double kayak before, you'll know that one steers while the other pedals/paddles and if you're not in sync, well, bad things can happen. And whether you know the person you're riding with or not, this scenario seems ripe and prime for communication breakdown.

We were floating down class-four rapids, and as we proceeded down the third rapid of the day, our boat caught an edge and flipped. Instead of floating down the rapid in a rubber kayak, we floated feet first, bumping into rocks, gulping down uninvited liquid, as the water moved so fast there wasn't time to think. Thankfully, we were both outwardly unscathed, but my inside world felt tattered, more shaken up and stirred.

At the end of the day, we stopped to set up camp alongside the river, and I ventured up river and sat down on the bank. It was the first time in months that I actually felt something as the water rushed by me. It was as if the water and I became one, as if the water washed away my insides, and I sobbed and cried. Something was unlocking at my core, releasing, cleansing, and letting go of deep pain, sadness, disappointment, and failure about what had become of my life, about myself. What I had thought was my dream life was now gone – it, too, being washed away and going down river.

After this experience on the river, I knew it was time to get off the Klonopin. It had been over nine months of medically numbing myself with prescription drugs, and I felt that after this river experience, I'd better do whatever I possibly could to get my life back on track or things may go south to a place I may not return.

I landed back in New York City a different person. I felt lighter, more aware, a little more back in my body, but definitely not fully. I called my doctor and told him I wanted to get off the meds, and he informed me of how important it was to not go cold turkey but to wean myself off. I followed his instructions, and as I came clean, I began to feel again. And what I felt wasn't always sweet. There was still a lot of pain, sadness, anger, hurt, and disappointment.

By the anniversary of 9/11, I had the realization that I needed to get out of New York City and that what was killing me was living there. I believed that if I physically removed myself from the place where my life was turned upside down, I'd be able to heal without drugs. But this was a classic version of attempting to rearrange the furniture of my life on the outside in order to try to make myself feel better on the inside. Unfortunately, this never works; as the old saying goes, "Wherever we go, there we are." Rearranging the outer world may give temporary relief, but eventually the pain from the inner world will again take over and life will become miserable.

Moving On

It took some time to sell my part of my business and tie up loose ends from living in New York City for almost twelve years, but I eventually moved to Montana, went back to school, thinking I'd switch careers and become an acupuncturist. My brother lived in Montana, and I felt I needed that drastic change from one of the busiest, most diverse, most cultured cities to Big Sky country, or what some might refer to as "God's Country" (from Manhattan to Montana, the only common denominator is the letter *M*). It was during this time, that my twin sister, who was always the more of a wuwu-guru type, discovered the Oneness University in India that was based on ending suffering for humanity. She transformed right before my very eyes and a few months before I was to begin acupuncture school, I decided to take my first trip to India.

It was a twenty-one-day course completed in silence. I think the longest I had ever stayed in silence up until that point was five hours. But twenty-one days? How was I going to do that? What I found was that the more silent I became, the more I was able to become aware of what was happening inside of me, which is where all of the magic lies. I learned that, especially in our culture, we do everything we possibly can to avoid what is happening inside, the feelings of discomfort, loneliness, not fitting in, not belonging, self-criticism, all of those unwanted feelings we try to avoid, we must go into.

The only way out is in.

And eighteen years later, after many trips to the academy for continuing education and living there for three years as a volunteer between 2010 and 2013 (another book for another time), I found the medication that actually worked to help get me through trauma and PTSD without using drugs.

But I must warn you: this medication is not for the faint at heart.

It is only for warriors.

Navigating through trauma and PTSD without the abuse of alcohol, drugs, or prescription meds is not an easy path where you can escape and avoid through pleasure. It is the path where you look deep within yourself to see what is actually there, what is keeping you feeling blocked, stuck, disconnected, and separate. It requires you to be authentic and honest and to accept what you see inside of you. It requires that you make commitment to awaken back to the natural state in which you were born. One of curiosity, wonder, joy, and fulfillment

If you're ready to say yes, then continue reading in order to find your own unique journey of healing trauma and PTSD without abusing alcohol, drugs, or prescription medication. I'll share with you what worked for me, and I'm convinced it'll work for you to.

CHAPTER 3
CHAOS TO CALM

Commitment to Trying Something Different

"We cannot solve problems by using the same level of thinking when we created them."

~ Albert Einstein ~

Okay, if you've made it this far, it tells me you are ready to commit to this process of healing trauma and PTSD without having to abuse (or use) drugs, alcohol and/or prescription meds. This next chapter will give you an idea of what is possible inside the scope healing ourselves by committing to trying something new, perhaps something we haven't tried before. It's a road map taking you from where you are today to where you want to be – which is perhaps living life without abusing drugs, alcohol, or prescription meds. Can you be open to trying something new?

Important Disclaimer

I must share with you a very important note: this process is not a substitute for taking prescription meds, for going to therapy, or for any other traditional form of treating PTSD and trauma. I am not a medical doctor, nor do I declare myself an expert at navigating PTSD and trauma without the use of prescription medication. But what I am sharing with you is the magic that worked for me to heal trauma and PTSD without the use of drugs. The reason why I chose to write this book and share what worked is to let other people know that it's possible. Because for me, it worked and it's long term. The medicine I am sharing with you in this book isn't something that takes you up, where you're feeling super "high" and all good, and then plunges you back down into feeling depressed, anxious, and disconnected. This medicine has a long-lasting effect that actually physically changes the brain and left me with a fresh, new perspective on life and how I choose to live it.

Post 9/11

After 9/11, I felt frustrated. I felt lost. I felt I was not in control of my body-mind, and I definitely had no connection to spirit. I left behind a life in New York City – what I thought was my dream life, which included an extremely successful business, loads of dear friends, and a fiancé, and decided to adventure out into the world to find a deeper meaning. From my experiences over the past eighteen years, I created a step-by-step process that has worked wonders for me, and I've seen it work for many others who I've worked with over the past several years.

Feeling Stable

The intention of this process is to bring us back to feeling stable. To feel strong and rooted in the body, to have courage and the strength to live with awareness, and to experience life again with a deep passion, with a connection to something greater.

The first step of this process is to stop.

We never stop. We never pause. We never give ourselves an opportunity for an internal "check-in" to see what is happening within ourselves. We are a culture who thrive on always being busy and who are constantly trying to become. It's almost as if the busier we appear to everyone, the more kudos we receive from the outside world, which, in turn, continues to fuel the ego, which, in turn, keeps perpetuating the same results of feeling unfulfilled, unhappy, and stressed, as if something in life is lacking or missing and your zest for life is lost.

One of my favorite quotes by Steve Jobs is, "If you define the problem correctly, you almost have the solution."

When you stop, it means you are admitting that you are in a bad place – where you are feeling stress, anxiety, pain, fear, anger, sadness, jealousy, comparison, judgment, blame, shame, guilt, worry, low self-worth, or whatever the bad feeling you are experiencing is.

Once you stop, you then observe: Where is the mind taking me? What is my thought process? Where are my thoughts taking me? Am I in the present, in the past, or in the future? You are not attempting to try to change what is happening, just simply seeing what is there.

The next step is to feel in the physical body where you are feeling or holding this emotion, this uncomfortable feeling. The body doesn't lie and will always tell you where you're holding it. Is it in your throat, your stomach, or your forehead?

One of my great teachers, Preethaji, says, "Our thoughts become our emotions.

Our emotions become our temperament. Our temperament gives rise to our innumerable responses that make or break a relationship."

We need to connect our thinking to our physical body. We hold it somewhere in the body, whether it's in the stomach, throat, head, or back. Wherever we feel stress or tension in the body oftentimes comes from our thought process. Where do you hold it? Feel it, acknowledge it, and name it. It is an emotion in the body wanting to express itself.

The third step in this process is to become familiar with techniques that help you to cultivate what I consider to be a Jedi Super Power: having awareness. You must become aware of how you always want to run, hide, avoid, and step away from any discomfort instead of leaning into it. The only way out of discomfort is by going into it. You must go through it. But instead, you've become so good at covering it up, using external means to try to avoid it, distracting yourself at all costs in order to avert what needs to be felt and experienced or else it ends deep inside your unconscious causing chaos, which we will discuss in a later chapter.

The fourth step is to be connected. Here, I will share with you techniques that help to cultivate more of those

Jedi Super Powers. When you feel connection in your life, you have freedom, an inner freedom. It's as if this inner freedom creates expansion that allows you to dance more freely, more wildly and without inhibition, judgment, or fear. It's not so much what great changes will be made in your external world but instead what changes will be in your inner world, your connection to yourself, which are then reflected out into the world and to others. And you do this by becoming more and more aware. Once you are able to become more aware of what triggers you, what makes you feel uncomfortable, you can become better equipped to handle yourself when you find yourself becoming derailed, off-kilter, stuck, or anxious.

To be connected helps you feel more stable, secure, safe, and strong. It gives you courage.

The fifth step is learning to let go and to forgive. If you don't forgive, you die a slow and lonely death. Lack of forgiveness is a poison and the more you carry around the resentment, shame, guilt, and judgment for what you may perceive the other did to you, the more this lack of forgiveness causes havoc and destruction to your body-mind and eventually to your entire world. It's as if you are drinking the poison by not forgiving but expecting the one who hurt you to die. For many of us who have experienced PTSD and trauma, this step can be very difficult and hard to comprehend depending on what our "story" is. You get attached to your story of hurt and trauma, and it sort of ends up defining you. Once you are actually ready to let it go, release it, and forgive, it can almost feel like a part of you is dying, and it actually is because you are releasing that which is no longer serving you; you are letting go of the old and you are making way for the new.

You are creating space for grace, for something alive, fresh, and more in alignment with who you are today, not from your past trauma or drama.

And the last step, the sixth step, is to elevate. If you are able to go through this process and not skip one part of it because you think you don't need it or because it makes you feel uncomfortable, then you will, in turn, elevate your consciousness.

This is why you get stuck. It is why you keep thinking the same thoughts over and over again. It's why you keep attracting the same types of relationships into your life over and over again, or you keep repeating the same destructive behaviors you have been for so many years. It's because you are not able to solve a problem from the same level of consciousness that created it.

You must elevate. We all need to elevate.

I will talk more about consciousness in a later chapter, but for now, know this to be true. In order for there to be change, you must see, feel, and experience what is inside of you.

Once you feel you're connected and elevated, it is imperative to create a vision for your life. A vision for where you see yourself in six months, twelve months, or five years. Having a vision for your life is imperative; otherwise, you are like a dry leaf blowing in the wind with no direction. Life happens to you instead of you creating the life you want.

Empowerment

Once you become comfortable with this six-step process, you naturally become more *stable*. You become equipped with tools to help you navigate and deal with PTSD and trauma symptoms, and the ways in which it affects your life. Instead of the PTSD or trauma making use of you and creating stress, turmoil, hurt, and pain, you take those emotions, turn them around, and make use of those feelings in an effective manner, using it as fuel for your own inner growth, transformation, and connection. I like to think of a phoenix rising and how, before it can rise, it must first burn all the way to the ground to ashes before being reborn again, before it is able to rise.

You have the capacity and the power to burn all of the hurt, pain, and trauma to ashes and be reborn again. It is taking what could be perceived as a big obstacle in your life and using it instead as an opportunity to create change. It is taking trauma, which can cause an extremely uncomfortable state, and using it as a gateway for transformation. It is what has the potential to *elevate* you, to bring you into a higher state of being where you feel connected to yourself and to everything around you.

The only reason we suffer is because we feel separate.

You no longer need to be the victim of circumstance but rather can be the one who is engaged in life, connected to life, manifesting and creating a life that you know you want to be living, the life you are meant to be living.

My Badge

When I left New York City and began my search for a more meaningful and purposeful life, I felt devastated. I felt weak. I carried my story around like a prized possession that gave me significance, a feeling of importance. The more I shared my story, the more it fed a part of me that needed to feel important, what we call the ego. What I came to know after many years of inner exploration, research, and study was that by letting go of that stinky old story, I was opening up the opportunity for me to feel internally free. But it couldn't just be a concept in my head of letting it go; it had to be an experience. It had to be felt in my body, either through an emotional release or through a practice of super-heightened awareness of what was happening internally in my body and in my mind (thinking) that would create this permanent internal shift, the elevation.

I hope this all feels doable for you. My wish is that this process doesn't discourage you, scare you or intimidate you, but instead inspires you, encourages you, and motivates you to begin to deepen your inner exploration of what may be keeping you feeling stuck with the trauma and PTSD, stuck in old patterns, behaviors, and destructive tendencies.

Sometimes in order to make change in our lives, we have to hit what some refer to as the bottom. I know for myself, I hit a version of my bottom after 9/11 where my life fell apart, and what I had once thought was important to me, no longer felt important, and life became meaningless. But things change, we change, life changes, and sometimes it happens so fast and without warning that it feels deeply traumatic and shocking to our nervous system derailing us. This process will help bring you back on the rails of stability, balance, steadiness, and alignment.

The most important step in this process is the first step, the step where we have to admit that we have gotten to a place of feeling we can no longer carry on in the way we have been, where everything we have been trying is no longer working – the traditional methods, therapies, drugs, and other means have for one reason or another, not worked and we feel helpless.

So, let's do a check-in of your life today and I invite you to be as honest and authentic as you possibly can be. No one will see this except you, so be true to you.

1. How do you feel about your relationships today?

2. Especially the ones with your mother and father?

3. When you spend time with your family, do you find you can only handle it for so long and then you find yourself wanting to check out? Run away?

4. Do you get triggered around your family? Friends? Or at work?

5. What are your triggers? What gets you fired up and stressed out?

6. What do you feel is lacking in your relationships today?

7. Depth? Authenticity? Acceptance of the other? The ability to listen? Honesty?

8. What are the three most important things to you in order for you to feel you have a fulfilling relationship?

9. Are these three things from your heart or do they come from a belief, a conditioning or from your upbringing?

Close your eyes and reflect on what you've expressed in your journal.

Imagine all of these people sitting together with you in a room. How do you feel? Take seven long, deep conscious breaths and see if you can allow yourself to be in the presence of these people even if they bring up uncomfortable feelings inside of you. Can you stay with the breath, stay present, stay grounded and trust that you are safe?

You'll hear me say this many times throughout this book: You need to begin the journey from where you are and not from where you think you ought to be.

There are many reasons why this first step of admitting where you are is the hardest step for most. No one wants to feel they are stuck or farther behind than other people. No one wants to admit that something might be wrong. No one wants to have to commit to doing any sort of practice in order to make it better. We all want a quick fix and to always feel good.

Follow this six-step process of getting *stable* and know that you are on your way to healing, from the inside out. From a deep well within that has the ability to nourish you on so many levels. No one gets left behind.

Let's begin.

CHAPTER 4
GET REAL ABOUT WHAT PTSD AND TRAUMA ARE

"Neurons that fire together, wire together."
~ Donald Hebb ~

In this chapter, I share a lot of facts and scientific evidence to help you better understand how trauma and PTSD can affect your life.

I would venture to say that pretty much every human being on this planet has in some way, shape, or form experienced a version of trauma. While our reactions to trauma may vary widely, and not everyone will develop PTSD from enduring a trauma; trauma is real and how it affects us can alter the course of our life.

What Is Trauma?

Trauma includes a wide spectrum of events and therefore can be hard to define. It can stem from a single experience or repeated events that overwhelm an individual's ability to cope or integrate the ideas and emotions involved in that experience. It can be direct exposure to an event, or caused by witnessing an event that causes stress, or it may be a more indirect experience, say by learning that a close relative or close friend was exposed to trauma.

Regardless of where the trauma came from, there are some common denominators:

- It was unexpected, which can cause shock to the body-mind-spirit.
- The person was unprepared.
- There was nothing the person could do to stop the trauma from happening.

Somebody once said to me, "Don't quantify your trauma," and I thought, exactly! Despite the wide spectrum of trauma, when it comes down to it, trauma is trauma.

Depending on your conditioning – how you were raised, your educational and religious background, your belief system – these things will determine how you react to trauma and how deep of an impact the trauma will have on you. It is very subjective. Falling off your bike for the first time and breaking your arm could be considered a trauma. Your parents getting a divorce could also be considered a trauma. Getting date raped at the age of fifteen could be a trauma. Living in New York City during 9/11 could be a trauma.

All of the above examples of trauma will have varying effects on your body-mind-spirit, depending on many factors.

Let's use 9/11 as an example to portray how the degree of separation from which you experienced an event will determine the extent of your trauma, the outcome. Your vicinity to ground zero will definitely determine how big or small of an impact the incident had on your system. Let's say you were running in Central Park when the first plane hit but didn't see it until you turned on the news thirty minutes later. Or maybe you were on the ninetieth floor of the second tower and made it out alive. Or perhaps you were a first responder who was at ground zero when the towers fell or a nurse in the ER of a nearby hospital that, within hours, was packed full of people injured by the attack. Or you had a spouse who was on Flight 93. Or you were camping in Yosemite National Park in California and didn't hear about 9/11 until four days later when you came back to the real world. All of these different scenarios will have varying degrees of impact that will determine how traumatic the incident was for you.

But no matter where you were on 9/11, you were affected.

"Trauma is when we have encountered an out-of-control, frightening experience that has disconnected us from all sense of resourcefulness or safety or coping or love."

~ Tara Brach, 2011 ~

When faced with normal levels of stress, the body will respond naturally with fight or flight where we are able to defend ourselves and/or move away from a situation that is dangerous or unhealthy. But when we are subjected to an extreme trauma, the body-mind kicks into freeze mode, and we get locked into feeling helpless, become paralyzed, and drop into failure of intelligence thinking we cannot save ourselves from what is happening.

What Is PTSD?

PTSD is a severe response to trauma where there is chronic stress following the traumatic incident. The body and brain are stuck in fight/flight/freeze mode, which is our natural protective mechanism that the body kicks into in order to adapt to a high level of stress. But if we are stuck in flight/flight/freeze mode, it can be both damaging and

FIGHT

- Crying
- Hands in fists, desire to punch, rip
- Flexed/tight jaw, grinding teeth, snarl
- Fight in eyes, glaring, fight in voice
- Desire to stomp, kick, smash with legs, feet
- Feelings of anger/rage
- Homicidal/suicidal feelings
- Knotted stomach/nausea, burning stomach
- Metaphors like bombs, volcanoes erupting

FLIGHT

- Restless legs, feet /numbness in legs
- Anxiety/shallow breathing
- Big/darting eyes
- Leg/foot movement
- Reported or observed fidgety-ness, restlessness, feeling trapped, tense
- Sense of running in life- one activity-next
- Excessive exercise

very straining on the central nervous system and other systems in the body and can eventually lead to anxiety, depression, and other diseases and disorders.

These days, when you hear someone talk or discuss trauma, you'll often hear the person speak about the importance of having a healthy, strong nervous system and why someone who has endured a trauma would benefit from this.

FREEZE

- Feeling stuck in some part of body
- Feeling cold/frozen, numb, pale skin
- Sense of stiffness, heaviness
- Holding breath/restricted breathing
- Sense of dread, heart pounding
- Decreased heart rate (can sometimes increase)
- Orientation to threat

The Nervous System and Why It's Our Gateway to Living with Jedi Powers!

One of my greatest discoveries after leaving New York City was finding Kundalini yoga – and I know some of you are saying, "Kunda-what?" Stay with me here, as I will be explaining more about this as we go along, but I want to share this very informative piece on the nervous system, its parts, and why it is imperative to have a healthy and strong nervous system.

According to Kundalini Yoga for the Nervous System by Nihal Singh, "The nervous system consists of three parts: Central Nervous System (sensation & motor control), Peripheral Nervous System (connects nerves to organs and limbs) and Autonomic Nervous System (emergency response: Sympathetic – 'gas pedal' & Parasympathetic – 'brake pedal').

"Some of the benefits of having a strong nervous system are that you can manage stress and be less nervous in tense situations. Robert Anton, in his book, Cosmic Trigger, wrote, 'We look for the secret – the Philosopher's Stone, the Elixir of the Wise, Supreme Enlightenment, "God" or whatever and all the time it is carrying us about… It is the human nervous system itself.'

"This is quite a profound statement about the nervous system. Here is one way to think about the nervous system: think about a child who watches a scary movie. The child anticipates something 'bad' is about to happen and looks away. The child cannot bear to watch what is about to happen. This is what a weak nervous system is like, in a way. A person cannot contain the reality of an event and therefore avoids it altogether. With a strong nervous system, one can watch and experience the scene no matter how painful. You cannot control what is happening on the TV screen, but you can control whether you allow yourself to experience reality.

"Another way to think about the nervous system is that it is a container. To some, their container is the size of a half-inch shot glass. This type of container can barely hold anything, so there is limit to the amount of stress or pain this person can hold. With this type of nervous system, it can be hard to even meditate for three minutes before feeling some sort of pain that will distract you. There is a limit to the depth of meditation one can experience with a weak nervous system as elevated states of consciousness can only be held for a short amount of time. It is said that people who have become insane from drug abuse experience high states of consciousness without a strong nervous system to support these states.

"One with a strong nervous system has a system more like a large steel barrel with the ability to hold whatever comes their way. This person can experience and process painful events faster as they can allow the experience without avoiding it. This person can experience more depth in meditation and can meditate for hours without distracting pain. When the nervous system develops the capacity to hold pain, then you can heal. You want to create the capacity to hold pain and then the system can bring awareness to it and then release it.

"We have become a society that seeks pleasure and avoids pain at all costs. I am not promoting masochism, but the reality of life is that there are good times and not so good times. By consciously avoiding the tough times, you are running from reality. We all do it on some level, but the truth is that avoiding pain causes neurosis. It is important to have a strong nervous system to be present and graceful during tough times. To be in the 'zone.'"

This is a fantastic description of why it is imperative for you to keep your nervous system healthy, strong, and vital and how, by having a strong nervous system, you can find yourself in stressful situations, and still be able to function with clarity, focus, and an intelligence, or a knowing of "what to do next" without slipping into freeze mode.

The higher the tolerance and capacity to handle the stress and trauma, the more effective you will be in helping not only yourself but also others when faced with stress and trauma. We'll talk more about this in Chapter 8, but for now, let's get back to the nervous system, trauma, and PTSD.

Think of your nervous system as being on a scale from zero to one hundred, zero being calm and in a neutral state; at one hundred, you're basically having a panic attack. When you wake up in the morning, your nervous system might be humming along somewhere between zero to thirty, but by midday – for many of us –you'll be surprised to know that you are probably running at about eighty or ninety. You'll know this is happening if you're starting to become irritable, tired, stressed, and anxious and are perhaps avoiding certain people or situations. This will explain why, when we are driving and someone cuts us off, we can quickly snap into road rage, screaming, yelling, and flipping off some random person we don't even know. It's because our nervous system is running at a high level of stress (remember, probably at eighty or ninety), and we need to do something in order to manage and calm the nervous system back down, targeting to get to that neutral zone.

The part of the nervous system that affects us most when we are experiencing trauma is the autonomic nervous system (ANS), which consists of two parts: the sympathetic nervous system (SNS) and the parasympathetic nervous system (PNS). The SNS is the part of the nervous system that protects us and controls the body's responses to perceived threats. The PNS is responsible for the "fight or flight" response. It controls homeostasis and the body's response "at rest." It is also responsible for the body's "rest and digest" function.

Again, this explains why we want to keep our nervous system healthy, vital, and running at a high function, so we are able to withstand when something outside our comfort zone, or out of our control, confronts us.

Before I found Kundalini yoga as a practice, I didn't know much about the nervous system and how greatly it can affect our state. Kundalini yoga is often referred to as

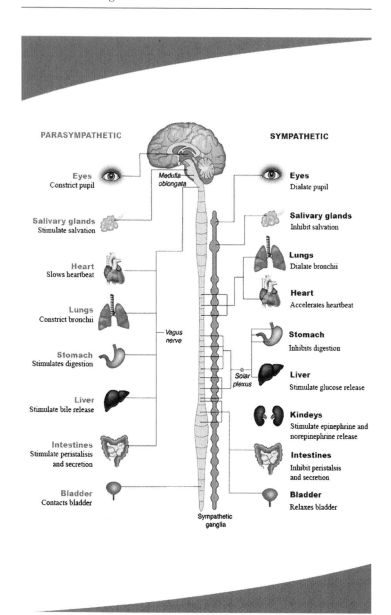

the "Yoga of Awareness" because it gives the practitioner ample opportunity to transcend the limitations of the mind through various forms of breath work, body movement, dancing, singing, and chanting (I know, it sounded really weird to me too at first, but trust me, it works). But after 9/11, I was looking for something that would help me become better equipped at staying more connected, more "present," more grounded in my body, yet still focused and coherent, even if I were to be confronted with something that felt way out of my control. That's how I found Kundalini yoga and experienced this for myself. I found that if I could commit to a daily practice where I focused and intended on clearing the passageways (i.e., the nervous system that fuels all other energy centers in the body), I could stay grounded, present, and very focused despite being in a stressful, painful situation or around people who were stressed, anxious, or uncomfortable.

I found out for myself that this stuff actually works!

And it's another one of the magical wonders that helped me change my life and get me off the meds.

How Do We Know If a Trauma or PTSD Is Wreaking Havoc?

Once the trauma has occurred, there are multiple ways in which the negative effects of the trauma or the PTSD can manifest, and this is when you need to be hyper-aware.

The negative effects could be physical, emotional, behavioral, cognitive, spiritual, neurobiological, or relational.

PHYSICAL

- Alcoholism or alcohol abuse
- Depression
- Illicit drug use
- Risk for intimate partner violence
- Multiple sexual partners
- Sexually transmitted diseases (STDs)
- Smoking
- Suicide attempts
- Adolescent pregnancy

BEHAVIOURAL

- Self-harm such as cutting
- Substance abuse
- Alcohol abuse
- Gambling
- Self-destructive behaviors
- Isolation
- Choosing friends that may be unhealthy
- Suicidal behavior

EMOTIONAL

- Depression
- Feelings of despair and hopelessness and helplessness
- Emotional numbness
- Extreme fear
- Guilt
- Shame
- Self-blame
- Self-hatred
- Feeling damaged or "bad"
- Anxiety
- Extreme vulnerability
- Panic attacks
- Compulsive and obsessive behaviors
- Feeling out of control
- Irritability, anger and resentment
- Difficulties in relationships

RELATIONAL

- Difficulty feeling love, trust in relationships
- Decreased interest in sexual activity
- Emotional distancing from others
- Relationships may be characterized by anger and mistrust
- Unable to maintain relationships

As you can see, there are numerous ways in how a traumatic event can affect you.

Most of us think there are only a few, but as we dig deeper into the understanding of this perceived injury, we can see how insidious trauma can be and how greatly it can affect your life.

COGNITIVE

- Memory lapses, especially about the trauma
- Loss of time
- Being flooded and overwhelmed with recollections of the trauma
- Difficulty making decisions
- Decreased ability to concentrate
- Feeling distracted
- Withdrawal from normal routine
- Thoughts of suicide

SPIRITUAL

- Feeling that life has little purpose and meaning
- Questioning the presence of a power greater than ourselves
- Questioning one's purpose
- Questioning "who am I," "where am I going," "do I really matter"
- Thoughts of being evil, especially when abuse is perpetrated by Clergy
- Feeling disconnected from the world around us
- Feeling that as well as the individual, the whole race or culture is bad

NEUROBIOLOGICAL

An overproduction of stress hormones that, when activated, do not return to normal, but can endure for hours or days as identified below:

- Jittery, trembling
- Exaggerated startle response
- Alarm system in the brain remains "on"; creating difficulty in reading faces and social cues; misinterpreting other people's behavior or events as threatening, sleep difficulty and the need to avoid situations that are perceived to be frightening
- Part of the brain systems change by becoming smaller or bigger than they are supposed to be
- Fight, flight, freeze response (which may look different from person to person)
- Responses are involuntary

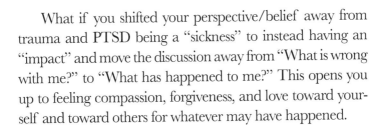

What if you shifted your perspective/belief away from trauma and PTSD being a "sickness" to instead having an "impact" and move the discussion away from "What is wrong with me?" to "What has happened to me?" This opens you up to feeling compassion, forgiveness, and love toward yourself and toward others for whatever may have happened.

The Magic That Is the Brain

And finally, let's take a look at how trauma affects the brain. While reactions to trauma can vary widely and not everyone will develop PTSD, trauma can change the brain in some predictable ways that everyone should be aware of, especially if you or someone close to you is struggling to cope after trauma.

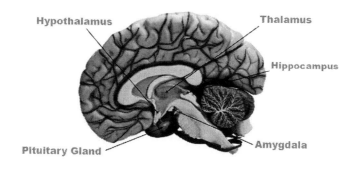

The area of the brain that we are going to focus on is the limbic system, the part of the brain that regulates emotions and memories. The three parts of the limbic system that are most affected after a trauma are the hippocampus, the amygdala, and the prefrontal cortex. The hippocampus is the part of the brain that takes us from short-term memory to long-term memory and is the "secretary" of the brain where all of our memories are filed. It is also what controls the ANS that we discussed earlier, the parasympathetic and the sympathetic nervous systems that regulate what we might consider as the "automatic" happenings in our body: breathing, blood pressure, pulse, and, don't forget, the fight/flight/freeze.

The second part of the limbic system that gets affected by trauma is the amygdala. The amygdala is our alarm system; it's what says "run" when you see a snake. Its primary job is to receive all incoming information – everything you see, hear, touch, smell, and taste – and answer one question: "Is this a threat?" If it detects that a dangerous threat is present, your adrenal glands produce the hormone cortisol, which raises your heartrate and blood pressure and kicks your body into fight/flight/freeze mode. We feel afraid, reactive, and vigilant, and we respond accordingly. The challenge when we experience trauma is that the amygdala becomes overactive and keeps us stuck in that fight/flight/freeze mode, which, as you can imagine, can eventually lead to anxiety, depression, and exhaustion. It's a lot for your body-mind to stay hyper-vigilant and on guard in search of threats all the time, and the stress will wear and tear your body-mind.

The third part of the limbic system that gets affected when you endure trauma is the prefrontal cortex, which is our thinking center. It is responsible for things like rational thought, problem-solving, personality, planning, empathy, and an awareness of others and ourselves. When this area of the brain is strong and healthy, we are able to think clearly, make good decisions, and be aware of our surroundings. But after trauma, this part of the brain can become underactive, which creates challenges in being able to navigate life rationally and with a clear focus.

The good news is this: the brain is pliable and therefore has the ability to heal itself. It is made up of plasticity, which allows the brain to get weaker or stronger. We will talk more about how to heal these parts of the brain in a later chapter, but for now, feel good knowing that this, too, has the opportunity to change!

"It's not the event that determines whether something is traumatic to someone or not, but the individual's experience of the event and the meaning they make of it."

~ Author Unknown ~

Journal Section:

This is where we need to become fully honest with ourselves because we can only begin the journey of healing from where we actually are, and not where we think we should be.

Where am I on the spectrum of trauma? (Remember, don't quantify!)

This is where we need to become fully honest with ourselves because we can only begin the journey of healing from where we actually are, and not where we think we should be.

What do I get from holding on to the trauma?

Who would I be if I didn't carry around this story about "my trauma?"

How would I feel differently?

And finally, start to think about who or what you might need to forgive for having had this trauma affect you and your life (and that might start with forgiving you).

CHAPTER 5
STOP, AND WHY THIS CAN BE THE MOST CHALLENGING STEP

Now that you've gotten a pulse on where you are "inside the trauma," we can start to get things moving. We discussed in Chapter 4 how trauma affects the brain and the various ways in which the trauma may affect our experience of life. We are moving into the actual process of what has to happen in order for this inner healing to begin. Let us begin by discussing what some might say is our biggest asset as a human being, but what also some might say is our biggest obstacle: the human mind.

Your Best Friend or Your Greatest Enemy

The human mind is extraordinary and very different than the brain. Its functionality is vast and wide-ranging, from cognitive faculties – including consciousness, imagination, perception, and thinking – to judgment, language, and memory. The mind bridges the gap from taking something that is entirely an experience and instead shifts it into a thought. It'll then go a step further and take it from being a thought to turning into an emotion. It's what tells you an orange is an orange. It's what gives you the capacity to debate on a topic. It's what allows you to have thoughts, as well as emotional experiences.

But what was an orange before someone told you it was an orange?

It was only an experience.

The challenge we are having with the mind these days is that it has taken over and is dominating our ability to feel, sense, or intuit our way through life. The mind only allows for thinking our way through; it doesn't allow for the component of feeling.

Allison

I remember when one of my clients, Allison, broke her leg. In one of our sessions, she told me how it all happened, how she cried, how badly it hurt, the immense pain she felt, and how she noticed that within a few minutes of her falling, the area on her leg started to swell, which began to alleviate the pain, (which is the body's natural way to respond and begin to mend), but then what happened?

Allison's mind kicked in, and the stories began to spew. She asked herself questions like "How am I going to be able to work?" or "Will I be able to still run?" or "What if I can't drive?" or "How will I get to work?" and on and on they went. The mind has the capacity to take you on such a journey. Allison shared how she ended up in a memory from when she was seven years old when her mom forgot to pick her up from school. Her mom left her waiting for an hour and a half before the principle realized she was alone and that no one had come to pick her up. She was afraid; she felt abandoned. She even questioned if her mother loved her because how could she have forgotten her if she loved her? And on and on the mind went with its stories that took Allison from being able to stay present with the broken leg to instead being in extreme psychological suffering that was triggered from when she was seven.

Where in the heck did this story come from?

Now you've gone from what has actually happened, you broke your leg, to a memory from your past that has taken you back to an emotion that has now got you feeling stressed, scared, and fearful; you're crying and feeling panic.

But wait. What happened to the broken leg?

New Science

Dr. Dan Siegal, a pioneer in a newer field of science called interpersonal neurobiology, says that we should reference the brain as a noun and the mind as a verb. When I heard this, I immediately thought, "Yes!" That makes perfect sense, as it allows me to better understand how the two function differently because the brain is a "thing" (a noun) while the mind is more of an "experience" or an "action" (a verb). For so long, we've sort of lumped the two together, the brain and the mind, as if they were somehow one and the same, but they are two extremely different realities with very different functionalities.

Dr. Siegal also says, "The human mind is, in a very real sense, much bigger and more expansive than the skull that we imagine to house it. What you do with your mind can even change the structure of your brain." Dr. Siegal and many other neuroscientists are now confirming that we are capable of changing the neural pathways in the brain from being negative (which could definitely stem from trauma) to more positive pathways. Remember, I said that the brain is pliable; there is plasticity, which means it can change. So, even if you've endured a trauma that created a neural pathway (or a deep groove in the brain) of negative thinking, stress, anxiety, or depression, the good news is we have tools and ways to be able to morph and change the brain back into something that reflects positivity.

How awesome is that!?

This gives us hope. This tells you that no matter what the trauma is that you lived through, you don't have to let it drive your life. We have the choice to say, "I want to live a healthy, happy, wonderful life. The only thing is that it will require me to do some inner fitness." I'll be sharing the "workouts" throughout the book.

The Mystery of Consciousness

Now, let's explore another trending topic that everyone seems to be diving into more of these days: consciousness.

There are three types of consciousness; there is the conscious mind, the subconscious mind, and the unconscious mind. Most of us are only aware of the conscious mind, of what is actually happening in front of us right here and right now. But what is indeed often running the show is our unconscious mind, the part of the mind where our memories, hurts, pains, and traumas are all kept nicely neat and stored (Allison's story of when she was seven). We keep these locked up deep down inside our consciousness and we operate our day-to-day lives often through these filters from the unconscious mind.

Let's say, for example, you grew up in a family where there was a lack of money. Your parents used coupons every week to shop. They lived paycheck-to-paycheck and food was rationed among the four kids, two parents, and the dog. Throughout your entire childhood until you became an adult, you always felt like there wasn't enough. There was this underlying sense of lack.

Then, you became an adult, went to college, went to grad school, and grew up to be a successful engineer, making $260,000 a year. You get married and have a child, only to find yourself every week combing through the newspapers looking for coupons, looking for the best deals on food that you know is not the healthiest for your body-mind-spirit, and yet you can't seem to shake the mental notion that there just isn't enough. You must save, you must cut corners, and you must constrict and contract.

Now don't get me wrong, we want to be mindful when spending our money and not be frivolous about it. But that's not what we are talking about. What we are talking about here is this prison you've created for yourself due to the conditioned beliefs and programming from how you were raised and how you grew up. This "conditioning" happens from listening to other people's beliefs, ideas, behaviors, interactions, and dogma. It can come from family, friends, religion, society, education, law. This is what is actually "running the show." And as a full-grown adult who no longer lives under those rationed, poverty-stricken circumstances, your actions speak otherwise. You've worked hard to create a new life for yourself, a life that consists of abundance and prosperity.

Then why this behavior?

This is the unconscious mind in action.

Some believe that we are only consciously aware of five percent of our thoughts, feelings, emotions, and actions, and the other ninety-five percent are coming from the subconscious or unconscious parts of the mind.

Let's now use an analogy to help us better understand the inner workings of consciousness and how it operates. Think of your conscious mind like the keyboard of a computer. You are typing and inputting information on the computer – this is what we could call the

conscious mind. We are constantly receiving input from the outside world through our senses, touching, feeling, talking, hearing, tasting, listening, smelling, seeing, and all of these experiences as if they are getting "typed into" the keyboard, which equals the conscious mind.

Next is your subconscious mind; this is like the software of your computer. It is where short-term memories are stored for easy access so you're able to navigate through your day-to-day life experiences with ease and accessibility. It's how we converse, problem-solve, plan, execute, and engage with the world. It's where we store and retrieve data.

Last, but not least, is our unconscious mind. This is like the hard drive of the computer where all the old files, memories, and programs are filed. These could be ideas and experiences from birth or childhood that we may never consciously think about, but that live inside the unconscious, and if it was a traumatic memory and we have not been able to fully experience it, we've managed to bury it using whatever means possible. It is as if it's still alive in the unconscious creating more of a mess in our day-to-day world than we probably give credit to.

Why Should We Become Aware?

"Awareness is the enemy of habit."

~ Sri Bhagavan ~

We are born and we grow up oftentimes not remembering how we are influenced by our birth, our parents, siblings, classmates, education, society, religion, partners, career, and before we know it, we are re-living either the exact same life our parents did or the exact opposite. If we grow up without cultivating a sense of awareness of what is happening inside ourselves, if we continue going through life stuffing all of the hurts, pains, and trauma deep inside our consciousness, it is literally like burying emotions alive that stay hidden beneath the surface like toxic waste bubbling as a radioactive negativity that seeps out throughout our day-to-day life whether we are aware of it or not. It's why we feel depressed and anxious. It's why we might snap at someone (usually those nearest and dearest to us) or have road rage. It's what causes us to "act out."

This is anxiety. This is fear. This is self-hatred.

The challenge is that we've become masters at escape, masters at covering it all up.

Some of us use drugs, alcohol, prescription medication, sex, gambling, shopping, or social media. We use anything to distract us from what is actually happening inside.

Stop for a moment and see what you are saying to yourself right now.

There is no need to beat yourself up about any of this or to feel any sort of guilt about it. Just see and observe, but don't try to change any of it; we are only trying to see.

Reflect for a moment on how automatic your life has become. From the moment you wake up in the morning – brushing your teeth, making your cup of tea or coffee

– think about how you do this without much awareness. You're basically going through the motions without being aware of what you are actually doing. As you do this, over and over and over, you are actually re-wiring the brain day after day, eventually living life with this sort of robotic behavior. Life suddenly feels like you are not living but instead merely existing. The joy, wonder, and curiosity of life fades away, and the day will finally come when you start asking yourself those existential questions like "Is this it?" or "Isn't there more to life than just this?"

In order to dig deeper into the unconscious, you have to be willing to go there and be a warrior. You have to do what I call having inner integrity. You have to be willing to see what you're holding onto, what is causing these blocks, the patterns, the repeated behaviors, and thoughts. Become aware of how the mind is making use of you by allowing the unconscious mind to run the show. You can become aware of this when you are able to see patterns in your life – destructive patterns that might include the same, repetitive type of relationships, or you may keep running into the same issues at work, or the same struggle with finances, any part of your life where you see a negative pattern. We need to clear out that unconscious part of the mind and make space for fresh reality to emerge.

Did I Wake Up on the Wrong Side of the Bed?

Georgia was a client who was physically abused by her boyfriend when she was fifteen years old, and eleven years later, she was still struggling with the ability to feel intimacy in her relationships. We started working the six-step stabilizing process when she shared with me that she was frustrated because she felt it wasn't working.

"I woke up the other day, and I just felt off," she said. "I instantly thought to myself, 'It's going to be one of those days,' and when I got to my car to head to work, I noticed someone had broken into my car. Nothing was stolen, but my car was a mess, and I felt extremely violated, which, of course, triggered fear inside of me and I panicked. I cleaned up the mess and started driving to work when my brother called. As we were talking, I realized I missed my exit, which made me twenty minutes late for work. I felt stress and panic again, and remembered the *Stable* process you taught me and began the deep breathing exercise we did. But it didn't feel like it was working, and by the time I pulled into work, I realized that I was supposed to be at our other location across town for a 9:00 a.m. meeting. The horrible day went on from there, but why didn't the deep breathing part work?"

Georgia forgot the first step, which is to stop.

When we don't stop – actually stop what we are doing – the "bad day" syndrome catches speed and inevitably everything seems to get worse and worse. When this happens, there is what I call a "failure of intelligence." Intelligence is different than intellect. Intellect is knowledge one accumulates throughout life from studying books, from reading, observing, doing research, et cetera. Intelligence comes from a different place. Intelligence comes from life experience, from being connected to something greater than oneself. Intelligence is what makes 300,000 starling birds fly in a beautiful, graceful formation without bumping wings into each other, where one leads until it's time to allow another to lead without competition, ambition, or neediness. Intelligence comes from being connected to something greater, some might call it being connected to consciousness, the Divine, a higher self, a Creator, or a God.

How do we do this? By having inner integrity.

This is another challenging part of the process: having to admit that something is off beat or feeling out of alignment. Some might say that something feels "wrong."

Why is this hard? Let's drop the why and just say, "This is hard."

It's okay.

You spend so much time trying to rearrange the furniture of your life in order to make you feel some sort of comfort. You want to make everything seem okay, where it all looks good and you attempt to be externally comfortable, thinking that, by doing this, it's going to make you feel better on the inside. You find new jobs, new partners, new clothes, new cars. You are constantly changing everything outside yourself, expecting that'll change how you are feeling inside.

You also spend so much time, energy, and effort trying to change what is happening internally. If you are experiencing jealousy, you do everything you possibly can to not have to feel that emotion because you judge it as being bad. If you are feeling anger, you try to hide it or stuff it down or act as if you are "not really bothered." You get stuck in the naming process, which is only another way to avoid what is really going on. What's that Bob Marley song? We're running and we're running and we're running away? But we've got it all wrong!

What you need to do is to focus, and put all of your energy and effort on your external world and into what it is that *you do* want in your life and stop trying to change anything that is happening in your internal world. Put your energy toward your family, your relationships, your career, and into your health.

And when it comes to the inner world? Become the observer and only observe what is happening inside. Just see. No doing, just being. But you have to stop in order to do this.

For many of us, the easiest and most accessible place to do this is by focusing on the physical body. We tend to hold on to our pain, trauma, and past in our physical body.

Julia

My friend Barbara asked me if I would be willing to work with her daughter, Julia, who was struggling and unhappy. Her high school boyfriend had cheated on her. He was her first true love, and the relationship ended in what felt like a huge heartbreak. But here she was, ten years later, and because she didn't have the tools back then or the means necessary in order to fully experience and express the feelings, thoughts, and emotions that erupted from having her boyfriend cheat on her, she stuffed them. She buried them. And they became part of the swamp pond deep down inside her unconscious that periodically (or perhaps more regularly) oozed out in dysfunctional, harmful ways. She now wasn't able to have a healthy, long-lasting relationship, and every relationship she found herself in, she ended up getting cheated on and couldn't figure out why. Julia felt like she'd built a wall up around her heart to protect herself, but it wasn't working. It was making things worse. She was having odd physical idiosyncrasies from heart palpitations to unexplained anxiety and had become a people pleaser just to keep everything seemingly "happy" on the outside, so nothing had to go too deep. She was suffering and couldn't find a way out.

We all find our magical, hidden ways to protect ourselves from having to feel.

But what is it that you are so afraid of feeling?

Out of control.

You believe that you are in control and the more you reinforce this belief through the ways in which you live your life, the more traumatic stress and shock are to your body-mind-spirit.

We live in a culture that puts an enormous amount of effort on external fitness, but what about the internal fitness?

We judge a mom in the grocery store whose two-year-old kid is having a meltdown temper tantrum and all we want to do is shut the kid up and make it stop. What would happen if we just let the tantrum run its course? What if, when you felt frustration, you were able to actually feel the feelings and allowed yourself to emote? Maybe shout, scream a curse word, or cry? What is wrong with that?

Instead, we've become more like Stepford wives; we've created an outer appearance that everything is so happy, even if, deep down inside, there is pain and disturbance.

There is mind disturbance.

We've all probably experienced at some point in our lives the "keeping up with the Joneses" syndrome, where we are constantly trying to achieve and do everything we possibly can to keep up with what we and everyone else perceives to be the "norm" in society. We end up doing things that are not in alignment with our values or aligned with our inner integrity just so we can feel significant or feel better than or more important. Know that we are dealing with the ancient brain, the reptilian part of the brain that is running the show and therefore, the behavior is also ancient. Now? We are upgrading.

Know that as you read this, you are becoming aware. Awareness is freedom.

I want you to take some time to get honest with yourself, to dig deep into your own truth of inner integrity, and see where you are today.

Is there a technique that will help?

Let's start by getting up and shaking your entire body, as if you are shaking off something that has been sprayed on you and you don't want to have on your body. Shake your feet, your hands, your hips, and your head, shake your entire body, and then sit back down again to read and then journal.

Ready?

Who am I right now in this moment? What is my inner state? Notice what emotions or feelings are arising inside of you. Is there fear, anger, rage, jealousy, or feelings of not being good enough? Just see what is there and don't try to change it. Just observe it. Do this for two minutes.

Now focus your attention by taking long, slow, deep breaths in and out through your nose and make the exhalation twice as long as the inhalation. Do this for two minutes.

1. Where do I see myself in six months?
2. Where do I see myself in one year?
3. Five years?
4. Do I want an intimate relationship with a partner, and if so (or if I already have one), what is important to me in this relationship?
5. How do I want to feel in this relationship?
6. What is important to me from the moment I wake up in the morning till the time I lay my head down to sleep?

For example, is organic food important to me or could I not care less?

Is reading chapters from a book everyday important or could I not care less?

What is important to you?

Be honest, real, raw, and vulnerable.

Be specific.

This is your time. Ask for what you want, what you need, all the big and little things that it'll take to create the life that you want, a life that doesn't include living through the veil of trauma.

CHAPTER 6
HOW THE BODY KEEPS SCORE

"Everything you need is inside of you."

~ Unknown ~

Step 2: Taking Inventory

Jackie was at the whim of her emotional reactions constantly. She came to me frustrated with her relationship, wanting to blame her husband for everything gone wrong. He didn't listen, things always had to be his way, and she felt she couldn't get a word in edgewise, especially when they were passionately disagreeing about something that felt important to both of them. She and her husband argued about which high school they were going to send their son to: her husband wanted their son to go to a private school, and she wanted him to attend a more alternative, creative, school. They seemed to be at a standstill, neither one willing to give.

When I guided her to go inward to see what she was feeling in her body, she said she felt tightness in her throat, a contraction making it hard for her to get a deep breath. As we continued to focus on the breath, bringing awareness to this place in her body, she remembered back when she was a young woman, about fourteen years old, wanting to attend a creative arts school, but her dad wouldn't allow her to. It wasn't open for discussion, and he shut down the conversation, leaving Jackie frustrated and out of control.

Throughout this process of becoming aware – first becoming aware of the contraction in Jackie's throat and then the shortness of breath – Jackie came to realize that because these emotions were not allowed to be fully experienced and processed when she was fourteen, the same emotions of feeling frustrated and out of control were getting triggered when she and her husband were having the discussion about their son and which school he was going to attend.

Jackie cried; she released the emotion and became aware of what was happening inside of her body and, in doing this, the wall of defiance that she was holding onto, of needing to be right, opened up the opportunity for her and her husband to come to an agreement about where their son would attend high school with more love, connection, and calm.

Our bodies are the most magnificent structures on the planet that are operating many systems all at once and at their own will. We don't even have to think about it much or put any effort toward it; it's just happening. Think about it, we don't ask our heart to beat – it just beats. We don't ask our digestive track to work out that salad or that Chinese food we ate— it just does it. It's automatic. It's nothing short of a miracle.

Let's go back to your dream, back to your vision. What is it that you want to see, feel, and experience from life? How do you want your relationships to feel? What do you want to give in your relationships and what do you want to receive? Hold those thoughts and visions inside of you, in your heart, and let us continue.

The easiest way to start building that inner muscle is by doing our "inner fitness," which is to be authentic and take an inventory of what is happening internally.

Pause and check your status:

If you are someone who has experienced a physical traumatic incident – say you were physically abused from a parent or a partner, or you were sexually molested or raped – then it might be too scary right now to bring your focus and attention (awareness) to the physical sensations of the body. If that person is you, then I want you to only focus on the breath.

Remember, baby steps. There is no finish line. There is nowhere to get to. We are all on a path together that never ends. No one gets left behind.

But Remember This: "The cure for the pain is in the pain." – Rumi

We must begin the journey from where we are, and not from where we think we should be.

Building inner strength is something that no one – and I mean no one – can ever take away from you. It's one of the reasons why it is so important in the recovery process and one of the most effective ways to rebuild those neural pathways in the brain that are more positive, uplifting, inspiring, and connected. But this takes time, patience, love, and compassion. If you're thirty-two, remember you've been living your life a certain way for thirty-two years and those neural-pathways are strong. If you're fifty-six, well, it's that much longer those neural-pathways have been groomed and formed. It's like a deep groove in the brain that the only way to reprogram is consistency, practice, and dedication to your growth and transformation.

Plasticity – We Have the Opportunity to Change Our Brain.

This first exercise I am going to share with you is called the Serene Mind Practice. This meditation is from a philosophy and meditation school in India called O&O Academy, which is where I study. At the O&O Academy, the co-founder, Preethaji leads us into the practice of Serene Mind as "our new superpower" to dissolve stress during challenging moments (more on that later).

You can do this meditation throughout your day, even at work! No one will even know you are doing it, and by the end of the three minutes, there will be a shift in your consciousness, in your nervous system that will bring you to a deeper sense of peace, presence, and connection.

If you are at work and can't do this at your desk, I recommend taking a break and going and sitting either in your car or, believe it or not, in the bathroom, where I have done it many times.

Quick but effective.

Serene Mind Practice

Have your timer out so you can time exactly how long for each part. If you don't have a smartphone, I'd recommend purchasing an old-school digital timer and using that because when we are intending to create an opening or a pause in the mind. We need to do everything we can in order to support that happening and setting a timer allows the mind to have one less thing to "think about" time.

Sit in a comfortable position where you can be completely still, not moving any part of the body, not itching or shifting or moving at all. Close your eyes (unless you are not comfortable closing your eyes — instead keep them one-tenth of a fraction open) and focus your gaze at one point in front of you. Keep perfectly still, and breathe long, deep, relaxed breaths. Have your exhale be twice as long as your inhale. One to two ratio breathing like this for one minute.

Bring your awareness and attention to the direction of your obsessive thinking. Are the thoughts pulling you into the past (regret, resentment, anger, hurt) or pulling you out of the present into the future (anxiety, worry, concern, fear). Think about this for one minute. This is taking inventory.

Don't change your thoughts or judge them, just simply observe and note whether they are pulling you into past or future. Do this for one minute.

Now for the last one minute, bring your focus on the area right between your eyebrows, some call it the agneya chakra, or the third eye center. See a flame of light in the center of agneya sending golden radiant light through the third eye and directly into the middle brain beyond it.

See this light piercing the center of the brain. See the center of the brain illuminated with golden light.

Come back to the space. Open your eyes. Notice what has shifted.

I've done this practice once a day and I've done it multiple times throughout the day if I happen to be having "one of those days." It works. But don't think that you'll do the Serene Mind Practice and everything will instantly become hunky dory. I'm going to keep reminding you about the brain and those lovely deep grooves that we are going to work on reorganizing or reprogramming throughout this process. I always tell my clients, slow and steady wins the race. There is no "quick fix," even though you might think that taking drugs, alcohol or those prescription meds that the doctor gave you would be a nice, quick fix.

I shared with you my story on how that worked – yeah, not so much. If you want the long-lasting stuff that works and doesn't require ingesting anything but more oxygen, then you're on the right path. Keep going!

Let's become more responsive and less reactive. Let's practice the art of inner integrity and become very authentic about what is happening inside of you.

The Body Knows

Moving deeper into the practice of awareness in the body. The body keeps a physical memory of all of your experiences. The body doesn't forget.

Remember that all of the various events of your life can leave physiological imprints in your body, especially when you experience trauma or situations of extreme stress, which cause the body to fight/flight/freeze in order to cope.

In a perfect world, you would be able to release the trauma or relieve the stress response soon after it was triggered (you'd shake!). Think of what an animal does after it gets into a fight. It shakes the body, as if "getting rid" of the trauma, which naturally calms down the nervous system and brings it back to a neutral state of homeostasis. Neutral state is where you want to be.

But we don't live in a perfect world, so instead, we are walking around with physical imprints of past experiences (good and bad) stored in our bodies. Most of us don't know how to release them because we don't even realize they exist (inner integrity)!

For example, you may feel your throat tense up when you have to ask someone for help with something you're not quite sure how to handle, or your entire body may tense up when you have to ask someone to borrow money, or your face may get hot when you're asked to speak in front of a crowd. These are the sensations in your body that you are remembering.

It's remembering a past experience when you asked for help and it didn't go well. Maybe someone made you feel ashamed because you "should be able to handle it yourself," or when you asked your dad for help, he made you feel stupid. Perhaps you were called to the front of your fourth-grade class and asked a question you didn't know the answer to, so you felt embarrassed and humiliated.

The body doesn't have words to express itself, so it responds with physical sensations.

You can forget, block, or intellectualize the memories that are stored in our brains, but how do you work through the memories being stored in your body? You might think you are successful at hiding it in your body, but then your back goes out, you get fibromyalgia, irritable bowel syndrome, or chronic fatigue.

The body doesn't lie, and it will eventually work the toxic waste you stuff one way or another.

Let's shift from destruction to restoration. Let's shift from self-hate to self-love. You've got the power to do this and only you.

I Am Courage

We are going to drop back into the awareness of our breathing. Pause and check your status. Remember to honor yourself and where you are at in this moment, and if you are not ready to focus on the physical body, then don't do it, just breathe. If you are ready, go to the next step.

Inventory Practice

Reflect on a time in your life when you felt embarrassed or ashamed, where your inner light got dimmed. Go all the way back to the time when you were young up until now. Do this for a few minutes, and as you are reflecting, as the memories start to come through, write down in your journal the various events where you felt guile, shame, hurt and pain from your past relationships.

Then, I want you to find in your physical body where you are holding the shame, guilt, and trauma, and begin to breathe into it. Bring the inhalation all the way to that place in the body, even if you're holding it in your knee, I want you to visualize the breath coming all the way down to your knee, creating expansion and opening in that space where there lingers constriction from holding onto that shame. Visualize a vibrant, shimmering golden light filling up that space where the pain, hurt, and trauma were. Do this for seven long, deep, conscious breaths and as you breath, see and feel that place expand, open up, and become alive again with vitality.

CHAPTER 7
ESCAPE, COVER UP, MASK, AND HIDE

Step 3: The Power of Awareness

"Change is inevitable. Growth is optional"

~ Sri Bhagavan ~

How does one become more aware? What does it even mean to be aware?

By taking baby steps.

During a one-on-one session, my client Patty shared how concerned she was because she had picked up her three kids from school the other day and came face to face with something that rattled her to her core. She spent about ninety minutes frantically running errands with the kids in the car, and as they were pulling out of the grocery store parking lot to head home, she suddenly realized she was going to hit the back end of another car. She slammed on the brakes, but it was too late. She smacked into the back of the car, and by the grace of

God, everyone was okay, but what made her panic was coming to grips with the fact that she had no idea how they got from Point A to Point B. Her head had been in a completely different space as she was planning, organizing, and ticking off her "to-dos" for the upcoming birthday party she would be hosting for their five-year-old daughter. She was completely not present or engaged while driving with her three children.

How could this happen?

You are gripped inside the mind and the mind is making complete use of you instead of you making use of it.

Has this ever happened to you? Where you suddenly realize you've been driving for thirty minutes and you have no idea how you got to your destination?

Remember, habit is the enemy of awareness.

How Do We Cultivate More Awareness?

You can begin to deepen and cultivate your sense of awareness by using that amazing, incredible, God-given temple of yours in order to experience life on planet earth, better known as "the human body."

Take something like the act of brushing your teeth, where you do put in your own physical effort. Even though you are brushing your teeth, are you actually aware while you are doing it? Imagine you are feeling the bristles on your teeth, tasting the peppermint toothpaste in your mouth, experiencing the salivary glands producing the saliva inside your mouth. Most of us do the act of brushing our teeth so automatically, without any sense of awareness of the actual touch, taste, or smell of the act itself, it happens, and before you know it, you are on to the next thing completely not experiencing anything having to do with the actual art of brushing your teeth.

Instead, you are off in another world, already at work, or at a meeting from yesterday, or perhaps making a grocery list for dinner or firming up plans "in your head" for what's coming up for the weekend. We "do" so much of our lives in automatic mode that for many of us, we've forgotten that we have the capacity to actually feel and experience every single act that is happening in every single moment.

This is a great depiction of the power of the human mind and the power of the imagination. This is what the mind is capable of in action. This is what is actually going on for most of us throughout our lives; where we are living in this automatic mode physically acting out our lives while simultaneously imagining a completely different reality that is taking place inside of our head.

We need our higher power to run our show and the only way we can do this is by practicing inner integrity, standing in our truth and leaning in.

It's time to lean in. Close your eyes. Take a deep breath and say to yourself, "I am safe. I am worthy. I am loved." Do this seven times. Trust the process. Pull out your journal and answer these questions:

1. What am I running away from?
2. What am I afraid of?

We run away from suffering. We run away from stress. We do anything we possibly can to avoid suffering.

Close your eyes and imagine you are perfect exactly the way you are right now. How does it feel to have zero judgment and only self-acceptance? Can you begin to believe this is possible?

Write your reflections in your journal.

What Is Suffering?

Suffering is what we call "carry over" from any past negative events that took place in our lives. It's the repeated thoughts that creep in from something from long ago (and long ago could mean five hours ago or five years ago. To me? They are both long ago!)

Suffering is when you resist whatever is happening inside of you; that, in itself, is suffering.

The mere resistance to what is, is suffering.

One of the problems is that you are constantly trying to explain your suffering or trying to understand it. It's that powerful mind that we talked about earlier that believes it can "think" its way through anything, including suffering or stress. But if this were true, wouldn't we all be bliss bombs walking around in ecstasy? The truth is, there is no thinking your way through the suffering, and there is only experiencing it.

You have to feel it. You must lean into it. Pause.

The hardest part of this process is actually seeing what is there. So often, when I meet people new to the path of inner growth and transformation, and they hear this concept of seeing what is there, their response is, "But there is nothing there? I feel fine." That is because we have become experts at running away from our suffering because to actually see it and admit that it is there can be painful. To look at your envious thoughts, your jealous thoughts, your fearful thoughts, your anxious thoughts, cannot be the greatest experience, so we, therefore, do everything we can to run away from it.

This is our problem. This is the problem of humanity. We need to lean into it.

Now, the mind will naturally say, "Okay, I'll lean into it because then it'll mean I'll never have another jealous thought, or I'll never feel fear." No, that is not right either.

Can you become aware of the jealous thought, the anger, the uncomfortable feelings?

Getting Comfortable Being Uncomfortable

I remember when I worked with a woman who had been physically abused by her boyfriend when she was sixteen. She completely shut down the "feeling" part of her physical body as a way to not have to experience the pain, hurt, and rage pent up in her body from being violated. The first time I asked her to close her eyes and begin paying attention to her breath, she panicked. She immediately felt closed in on and her breath became shallow and rapid. I invited her to stay with what was coming up, to deepen her breathing, and to continue staying with what she was feeling in her body. She described how her breath would go only chest deep and that she was too afraid to take it any deeper. I assured her that was fine but told her to stay completely aware of the physical sensations that she was experiencing: as she inhaled, feel the cool air enter her nostrils and her chest expand, and as she exhaled, feel the warm air exit her nostrils and her chest soften.

It doesn't matter how big or small the awareness is; becoming aware of any of the physical sensations will help to build this inner muscle that we all need more of in order to shift from feeling separate to feeling more connection. My client didn't need to have an emotional outburst in order for growth to occur; her growth for that day was paying attention and being aware of her breath, to the physical sensations in the body and that was enough.

Can you actually soak in the discomfort and not move away from it? Can you find your breath, connect to your body, and open up to it instead of resisting contracting and moving away from it? Since when did we say that in order to be happy, healthy, and holy we have to constantly be comfortable? That is a conditioned belief that our culture has greatly fed into and almost forced into believing is true. You can see it when you look around you and everything is super-sized and anything and everything is at your disposal, anytime – fast food, fast coffee, fast relationships, because as soon as they start to feel uncomfortable, we find enough blame to say, "I'm out. This isn't for me." We do everything we possibly can to be cozy, comfy, and surfacey and not run too deep.

Lean In, Go Deep

I've had people say to me, "Okay, but if I am in a relationship that is verbally (or physically) abusive, do I stay in it? Are you telling me to lean into it?" And the quick answer to that would be no, but before you run away from it, let's dig into it a bit further. If somebody is verbally abusive to you, can you pause, breathe, and look to see what it is bringing up inside of you? What are you feeling? Where are you feeling the contraction in your body?

Can you, instead of blaming and pointing the finger at the other, lean in and look to see what it's bringing up? Are you able to confront it? Initially, this could be very difficult, scary, and uncomfortable, but after you do it a few times, you start to feel a release and the opening that occurs from leaning in versus running away becomes delightful. It's what gives you that inner power, that inner strength.

The reality is, you're going to bump into self-doubt or self-judgment, maybe even self-hate at times. But once you see what is there and accept what you are experiencing, something will begin to shift. You will literally go from this suffering state into a state of complete joy and bliss. The suffering is contracting; the acceptance is expanding. Contraction is fear. Expansion is joy. You may even get to a point where your partner is yelling at you, and because there is nothing inside of you that the yelling is triggering, you are able to stay present and aware, and the experience may actually become blissful.

Can you be comfortable inside the discomfort? Can you allow for whatever is there in every moment to be there? Can you stop running away and instead lean in?

We all have this sort of fantasy of what it means to be a human being – this unrealistic expectation of ourselves to being only light, good, happy, and pure. But the reality is that we live in a dualistic world that has both sides to the coin of what it means to be human. You have good. You have bad. You have black. You have white. You have joy. You have fear. You are the full spectrum of humanness. It is your response to this perceived perception of having a "negative, dark side" that makes or breaks your steadiness, your inner strength and your radiance. You think that if you keep pushing away the negative, you will be radiant, but the opposite holds true. If you are able to allow for it, honor it, acknowledge what is there, that is what will bring radiance. Truth equals radiance. Acceptance equals your beautiful human grace. Truth is the first step in spirituality. From there? Everything becomes automatic. Stop trying to be perfect and instead be who you are in each moment. Honor that. Respect that. Allow for that.

Perfectly Imperfect

Close your eyes and imagine you are perfect exactly the way you are right now. How does it feel to have zero judgment and only self-acceptance?

We believe we are always trying to get somewhere. We are always trying to change and become. But what if there is actually nowhere to go and there is nothing we can actually do to change except to see what is there? If you are a jealous person, you are not going to become a non-jealous person. If you are a fearful person, you are not going to become a non-fearful person. If you are a sad person, you are not going to become a happy person.

The mere thought that you can and should change is what is causing you suffering. It is causing you inner turmoil, mind disturbance, and stress.

Feel into this:

You cannot change. There is no need to change because you have been designed to be just as you are and that is perfect! You are that. Accept who you are, just as you are, and stop trying to change. You did not design yourself. The Creator designed you to be just like you are, and there is some purpose in that design. Acceptance is the freedom. Embracing yourself as you are is what is important. You are unique. God/Creator made you this way and that is that.

The more we try to push away the negative thoughts and emotions, the stronger they get. The more you resist, the more they persist. The more you fight, the stronger they become. The only way is to see what is there and accept them, and then they become weaker.

Suppose you believed that if you could make your heartbeat have a different rhythm than what it naturally does, you could become an Olympic runner. What would you do to make that happen? How would you make your heartbeat change? You couldn't. There is nothing you could do. You can't change your heartbeat. It is what it is. The same goes for your emotions and feelings. These are part of being human. Jealousy, comparison, doubt, judgment, these are part of the human experience. But because we resist them, because we believe we shouldn't feel these things, they get stronger and stronger eventually creating a mess in our world causing anxiety, depression, self-hate, and other disease.

After 9/11, a fear grew inside of me that I was no longer safe in public places. I loved using the subway when I lived in the city and it was my preferred means of transportation. But after 9/11, I experienced great fear every time I'd venture down to catch a train because all I could think about was chemical warfare and how one of these days, someone was going to seep some chemical into the subway system and we'd all die. My heart rate would speed up. My palms would get sweaty. I'd nervously look for unusual activities. I'd feel stressed. These thoughts of chemical warfare were what I believed to be "my thoughts." So, I decided (like many of us did) to stop using the subway and instead, to use taxis, car services, and buses. It was safer above ground.

Herein lies everyone's fate who starts changing the external world in order to try to make the inner world feel better. It is the start of your world closing in on you. In order for you to feel safe, secure, and "okay," you start cutting things out of your life: maybe it's using the subway, perhaps you start avoiding people who make you feel uncomfortable, or maybe it's your favorite coffee shop because a worker who works there triggers something uncomfortable inside of you. You start building walls around yourself, and eventually you are guaranteed to be living in a black room, with a black cat, drinking black coffee all alone.

You isolate, and when you isolate, you are disconnected, and when you are disconnected, you suffer.

What if you didn't have to cut anyone or anything out of your life and could still feel safe? You can. But you have become aware of the discomfort, lean in to those feelings that you keep running away from. The more you lean in, the less impact the discomfort will have on you each time. Shall we try this?

Journal:

1. What does your heart know to be true that your head does not want to admit?

2. Who would you be without the trauma? How would you feel or be different?

3. What are you afraid of? Does that fear really serve you going forward?

4. What past stories, traumas, hurts, and pains no longer serve you in your life that you are ready to release and let go of?

5. What would you do differently if you knew no one would judge you for it?

6. Name something you used to love but had to give up after the trauma? How might you invite it back into your life?

7. Can you allow for whatever trauma happened to you, to just be there? Can you make space for it, room for it? Can you allow it? Can you breathe into it?

8. How does that feel?

Now visualize a huge, golden orb of light right above your head. It's radiant, pulsating with energy, alive, and full of power. If you are ready, invite this golden orb of light to descend down into the crown of your head. As it touches the top of your head, take a deep breath and continue to invite it deeper into your being until it resides in the center of your chest, your heart center. Take three deep breaths, and with each breath, feel that golden light anchor into your being, as if it is lighting up all of your cells with this radiance, this beauty, this power. Now ask your higher self to show you where in your body you hold the trauma, the stress, the pain, the hurt.

The mind is going to come in and try and take you somewhere else or say it doesn't exist or why am I doing this. Acknowledge the mind, and say, "Thank you, but I've got this," and then go back to the breath and asking to see where the pain is being held. Once you find that spot or that story, I want you to feel it. Experience it. Breathe into it. Allow it to be there and ask it to reveal to you what it needs in order to merge and become one with you. Not to reject it or push it away, we want this carry over of pain to merge within our cells and become one with our entire being. Feel this happening. Thank your higher self for showing you this. Thank this Golden light for helping you merge this pain and trauma.

Bring your palms together in front of your heart space, bow your head and say thank you.

Express gratitude.

CHAPTER 8
THE METHOD

Step 4: Be Connected

Now that you've reclaimed some of your power, let's continue forward in this process of becoming a whole human being again. I shared with you earlier about a semester abroad I experienced with my "little sister" Brooke in Florence, Italy, studying art, literature, and landscape design. One of the many tours we took during that semester abroad was a trip to Rome where we got to tour the Vatican. You can imagine the excitement, curiosity, and thrill of walking into the Vatican for the very first time. As we entered the Sistine Chapel – or what felt more like the heavenly realms with great depictions of ornate altars, Adam and Eve, Noah and his ark, angels, prophets and lots and lots of soft, curvy portrayals of naked bodies – I will never forget the feeling I felt. It was as if my breath had been taken away. Tears rolled down my face and I felt such a presence take over my entire body that felt like a wave of grace. I guess you could say

I felt love – unconditional love that had no meaning or purpose, just pure love. I felt connection.

What I later realized was that this feeling I experienced birthed from what had been so consciously and lovingly put into that space for centuries and centuries. It began with the famous Renaissance artists, Botticelli, Rosselli, and Michelangelo, who poured their hearts, souls, and love into each painting that covered the ceilings and walls of that benevolent space. Each one of the fresco paintings was alive with a presence, a sacred energy that left one curious with wonder, like a child. The colors, textures, designs, and curves created a sense of connection for the observer and the observed. That wave of indescribable feeling came from the amount of prayer, ritual, meditation, and honoring of the Divine that took place in that space, which automatically brought huge respect and the utmost integrity.

It was visceral. It felt alive. Hence the tears. I guess when you're an empath (someone who feels their way through life), there was no stopping the feeling; it overcame me.

Why do I bring this up? Because I want you to have a piece of the Sistine Chapel in your home. I am inviting you to create your own sacred space either in your home, apartment, car, at work, wherever it is that you feel you need some tranquil peace, a place of refuge, to refuel, reenergize, nourish, connect, and practice.

Right now, there is an opportunity for you to pause, and ask, "Do I want my children to be a part of this space? Do I want my partner to be involved? Or does it feel more nourishing at this moment to create this space for myself knowing I can always change my mind later on and invite others in.

But perhaps for now, it's just mine.

Let us now look at the word sacred and the various meanings that it embodies from two different perspectives.

On a macro, universal scale is when we see in the bigger picture combining all different aspects of the "sacred" as one. Sacred in some traditions means cleanliness and purity and no swearing, gossiping, thinking ill thoughts, or violence; it creates a sense of peace, quiet, stillness, expansion, reverence, a web of existence that connects all things. Sacred is holy, divine, auspicious, and some say it is connected to books, music, or religion.

From another perspective, the micro scale, sacred is unique to each individual and what he or she declares as sacred. What might feel sacred to one person may not feel sacred to another. That's okay. Whether you are Christian, Muslim, Jewish, or Hindu, come to realize within yourself what sacred means, what sacred feels and looks like.

Take, for example, indigenous cultures and other ancient traditions where the term sacred was a very important part of one's life. As we have evolved, a lot of humanity has moved away from sacredness – and evidently lost touch with its true essence. Now, as we begin to understand the importance of sacredness in our day-to-day lives, it can be hard to know where to even begin.

Sacred means being connected.

Creating sacred space can and should be fun. Even if you hate anything and everything creative, it doesn't matter because this is your sacred space and is only going to reflect you, what you like, and what makes you comfortable. You want your space to be inviting, to call out to you, to entice you so that you stay committed to your practices. Do you like candles, essential oils, crystals, feathers, tarot cards, incense, fresh flowers, clothes or rugs, rocks, or photos? Are you a person who likes lots of things scattered about or are you simpler and more minimal?

When creating sacred space, bring those sacred beliefs, thoughts, ideas all together into a space and see what reveals itself. My personal sacred space has a pretty white cloth, fresh flowers, crystals, an orchid, candles, incense, statues of deities, photos of orbs, golden balls, feathers, and other pretty things. This symbolizes sacred to me and is unique to me, only. What makes you feel sacred?

Creating a sacred space is like building any other relationship. It'll give back to you whatever it is that you give to it. If you create this space and you only sit there once a month, it'll become another area of your home that collects dust and cobwebs. But if you want this space to feel alive, to have presence as I felt in the Sistine Chapel (yes, you can have this), then it'll require your energy and your attention for you to constantly be changing things around, dusting it, bringing fresh new flowers, new candles, et cetera.

You can bring sacredness to any part of your life. You can offer thanks at every meal to all those who put their hands and hearts into bringing that meal to your table. You can feel sacredness when connecting with another human, whether it is listening to someone share about what is going on for them and holding space or perhaps when you're making love to your partner you can feel sacred. Remember that much of our lives have become robotic and automatic and one of the tools that'll help you cultivate that awareness is bringing sacredness to as many parts of your life as possible.

Sacredness = Awareness = Freedom

A dear friend of mine, who is seriously obsessed with anything sacred, has her entire house filled with various pictures, statues, symbols and representations of the Divine, where you literally feel that presence, that connection I spoke about earlier when we were inside the Sistine Chapel. You walk up to the front door, and there are two statues on either side of the door, one of the Mother Mary and the other of QuanYin. Both are laced and adorned with these outrageously fat, fluffy, soft, exquisite, colorful, fresh roses that are replaced every single day. Then, you step inside her house, and everything is pristine, has its place, where you feel and experience this reverence, honor, and respect for the sacred. Whenever I go there, I feel as if I've been purified by Divine energies as they wash away any fear, suffering, chaos or doubt.

We all have the capacity to have this in our home. It's up to you how much time, energy and space you want to put into your sacred space knowing that what you put into it is what you'll get back.

Connection to something greater than yourself is key. It's where the magic lies. Create something that draws you in, that reminds you of this very important aspect.

Creating Your Own Sacred Space

If you are ready to make a commitment to maintaining a sacred space in your home car, office, or wherever it is that you want or need it, then now is the time to do that. Find a place where there won't be distractions, where there won't be a lot of traffic or noise, and a place where you can call your own. Close your eyes and begin to focus on your breathing, taking the breath deep into the belly, expanding the breath to all parts of your body. Now begin to visualize your sacred space. What would you put there? How would you want it to feel? Would you have a little table with a cloth on it? What color is the cloth? Are there flowers? Candles? Incense? Essential oils? Maybe a picture of a statue or of a deity? Tune into what makes you feel comfortable and what allows you to soften and feel a connection. Once you have the vision, you then have what it takes in order to create this space in your home. Remember, having sacred space is like any relationship, it requires your energy and your attention. If you create sacred space and then not sit there for a month? It'll collect dust and it'll feel dusty. But if you sit there every day, even if it's only for two minutes? It'll feel alive and it'll become more and more inviting for you.

CHAPTER 9
THE PSYCHE OF EGO

Step 5: Let Go and Forgive

We have all experienced a version of trauma in our lifetime. It could be your mother leaving you with your alcoholic, abusive father when you were three years old, or an uncle who sexually abused you between the ages of seven and eleven. It could be when you walked in front of your high school classmates of 1,250 people at graduation, tripped, and fell and your skirt flew up over your head, showing all your private parts. Or maybe you had a son or a daughter who was killed in combat. Or you are a first responder who sees tragedy and death day after day after day after day. The spectrum of trauma is vast, but when it's your own story, your own experience, it is hard not to think or believe that your trauma is somehow the worst one of all.

Remember Not to Quantify. It's All Trauma.

Let's face it, any sort of trauma or PTSD stinks, and again, if we lived in a perfect world, we wouldn't have to talk about this topic and how to handle it. But we don't live in what we perceive to be a perfect world and many of us do endure some sort of trauma or PTSD, so here we are, figuring out a way to navigate through it without having to abuse drugs, alcohol, or prescription drugs.

Going deeper.

Struggle is what creates beauty.

Everything Has a Crack in It, but That's Where the Light Gets In!

One thing about life that is guaranteed is that it has ups and downs, and we can always count on having more. You've probably noticed by now that life brings you to your knees, and oftentimes it brings you lower than you think you can go. But if you stand back up, and continue moving forward, if you go even just a little bit farther, you will always find love.

Love is at the core of every human being.

Now, some of you might have a hard time reading this next part, but it has been such a profound insight for me, so much so that I can't help but share it with you.

Let Your Consciousness Get Bigger Than the Problem

What is collective consciousness? We talked about individual consciousness, the conscious mind (keyboard), the subconscious mind (the screen and short-term memory) and the unconscious mind (the hard drive). Each species has its own collective consciousness. There is snake consciousness, bird consciousness, bear consciousness, human consciousness. This explains why when you think of your great-aunt Betsy who you haven't talked to in two years, five minutes later your phone rings and it's her; that happens because of the collective consciousness. That happens because of the interconnectedness of everything.

Since I am a visual person and having an image helps me better understand ideas and concepts, I like to think of it like this: Consciousness is like our nervous system with all of the different strands connecting us all. At the end of each strand is a neuron, which could represent a human being depicting the interconnection of humanity meaning we are all connected no matter where we are on the planet. It's like a giant spider web of connection. I am you and you are me. We may all look different, but we are all one, meaning we all come from one place; we are all connected.

Now, imagine an emotion-sphere. All of the emotions that you are unable to process and experience get put into this emotion-sphere. I keep bringing up the toxic waste bin, but that's really what it is, and these stuffed emotions get collected inside this emotion-sphere. Now imagine there are one of these emotion-spheres for the collective consciousness as well and all of the emotions that each individual is not able to experience gets not only put into the individual emotion-sphere but also into the collective emotion-sphere.

For example, you and I experience anger in our own, unique ways and for different reasons, but we both experience it from time to time. I experience jealousy and you experience jealousy at different times and in our own unique ways (and anyone who says, "I don't ever experience jealousy" needs to run in the other direction because they are living next to the largest river in Egypt – better known as "denial"). These are human emotions we all experience no matter what. Even the enlightened sages experience these things, but what makes them enlightened is that they do not resist whatever it is that comes up and instead are able to fully experience the emotion. They don't stuff it, hide it, or pretend it doesn't exist. They don't cover it up with booze, cigs, weed, or prescription meds. It's just there; it is felt, and it moves on.

Grow Your Way Out of It

If I don't allow myself to feel the negative emotions, and I stuff them, where do they go? Into the toxic waste bin of my unconscious (i.e., the emotion-sphere). Check this out: that also gets added to humanity's collective consciousness and every time a human being does not allow and experience their personal emotions, it gets put into the individual septic tank but also into the collective septic tank. For individuals, it'll eventually show up as a disorder or a disease: anxiety, depression, colitis, arthritis, chronic fatigue, cancer, et cetera.

But for the collective? It shows up as 9/11, the Orlando nightclub shooting, Columbine, the Route 91 Las Vegas shooting on October 1. It literally is like a balloon popping that releases the pent-up negativity that was unable to be experienced on an individual level and therefore got put into the collective pool of toxic waste that eventually has to get released somehow. It's nature's law. We can't keep blowing hot air (anger, fear, pain) into the balloon and not expect it to eventually blow.

When I first heard this, I resisted it. I thought how could I have anything to do with 9/11? That's ludicrous. And yet, the more I thought about it, the more it started to make sense, and what I found was instead of me feeling like the victim that has no control, I suddenly started to feel empowered, believing that I could actually create change and affect the collective if I did my own inner work. This inspired me to go bigger and deeper into my devotion and dedication on the path to growth and transformation.

I remember after 9/11, I felt so frustrated because I felt like I couldn't really do anything. I wanted to help, but didn't know how. At that time in my life, the only way I thought I could help was if I became a lawyer or a politician, and for a fleeting second, I actually thought about doing it. But that idea quickly came crashing down as the reality set in that to be a lawyer or a politician just wasn't me. And then I'd feel frustrated again. Back to feeling like I couldn't affect any change or have any impact. But after I heard this teaching/insight about how the individual affects the collective and that if each one of us does our inner work of staying with what is really happening inside of us in each moment, not running away, not avoiding what is there, that this would, in turn, affect the collective consciousness and not feed into those massive tragedies.

Okay, well if this is true, then how do I catch myself before I make the decision to run, hide, avoid, distract, or cover up?

You become aware of the games you play within yourself and with others. You become aware of how you get trapped inside what's called, "The ego games."

Paul came to me frustrated and ready to let go of his six-year relationship with his girlfriend. He'd had it. He was so tired of him and his girlfriend arguing and more than that, how she never could see his side if the story. He hated that she always had to be right. Why couldn't she just see his side of the story for once? Why did she always have to be right?

The Ego Games?

There are six games we play using the ego, and, again, for most of us, it is unconscious. We are not even aware that we are playing these games, but they are often running the show and create destruction. The more we learn about these ego games and how they work, and practice becoming aware of when we drop into them, the healthier our relationships and more fulfilling our lives will be.

I often hear from clients, especially those who live and work in the corporate world, who say that if we get rid of the ego, how will they be able to debate in a corporate meeting or how could they become a doctor? The fact is this:

The freer you are from the ego, the more successful you will be at whatever it is you are doing.

We have to differentiate between the self and the ego. Think of self as an ambition – the self has the will to fight it out or the will to achieve. We are not talking about the self as we would definitely need drive and will to make it through medical school. But the ego, on the other hand, makes you positional and when you become positional, you don't understand what the other person is trying to communicate and have failure of intelligence.

Think of a time when you were having a conversation with your partner, friend, or co-worker, and the conversation escalated because there was a disagreement between the two of you. Once the disagreement appeared, you closed down. Your body contracted, constricted, and you no longer were able to listen to what the other person was saying, but instead you conjured up what your response was going to be and/or the trigger had your mind lost in some story from the past.

Because of this, there is no learning about the other or the situation at hand, and therefore you have every chance of losing. You have every chance of losing a friendship, a good employee, connection, or a business deal. You have every chance of losing a good insight. This is how the ego proves to be very harmful to corporate success as well as your relationships with others.

I am not talking about the self. It is important for the self to stay intact if you want to achieve success in the world. I am talking about the ego and the games that the ego plays that can be very harmful in the process of achieving success. What we need to do is learn how to distinguish between the two, between the self and the ego.

These Are the Games We Play

1. Dominating Others:

Domination of others is a natural game in order for the ego to survive. We normally dominate others by saying that we are parents, spouses, leaders, employers, officers, heads of the family, et cetera. Our position as parent or a leader gives us the excuse to dominate others frequently. We use this stance most often in the pretext of concern for the organization we are working for or as in concern for the other person, but our mind subtly allows us to dominate others. More often, we are unaware of this subtle interference of this ego in many of our relationships.

2. Refusing to Get Dominated

We need to also understand clearly that it is the ego that refuses to be dominated. This is another subtle and dangerous game that the ego plays. If we do not have an ego, why should we resist if another person is dominating us? In the absence of this ego, we will happily surrender to domination by others. But most often, we do not like to be dominated in any way. We need to understand that this is nothing but the ego playing inside us.

3. I Am Right

The ego in us will always want to prove that "we are right." Again and again, we argue and try to prove that we are justified or right. There will be a lot of explanations in order to prove this. We should be aware of this ego game when we are trying to prove that we are right.

Why should we never prove that we are right? If we are actually right, there is no need to prove it. Nature, the universe, or some might call it "God" (you can name it whatever you want – light, creator, Divine, creation, et cetera) will always prove for us that we are right without us having to say or do anything.

If we become aware of this game of the ego inside us and admit that it is there, it will always be shown organically (without our effort) that we are actually right.

4. You Are Wrong

This is the other side of the coin. Just as we feel the need to prove that we are right, we also want to prove that the other person is wrong. This is nothing but the ego playing its game inside us.

These games are extremely insidious, and you have to be ultra-aware and authentic in order to admit that you are playing them. But once you do, it becomes fun.

5. Survival

Ultimately, the ego, in order to survive inside of us, will simply lead us into thinking that it is playing none of these games. The ego will always justify itself. The mind will lead us to think that we are not all bound by ego or we are absolutely right in our egotistic approach.

6. Cover-Up

Often, we cover up our ego by commenting about the other or finding fault with the other. We should be aware that it is this the ego and hurt that is more often finding fault with others. Here we are not talking about practical and functional faults. We are talking about characteristic judgments and blaming and labeling others.

These are the six games played by the ego. The more you understand them and see them in action, the healthier and more fulfilling your relationships will be. When Paul learned these six ego games, his arguments went from being frustrating and devastating to being more manageable and sometimes even entertaining. He saw how he became the victim and she the perpetrator and how those were the "go to" roles they fell in to. Once he played with these ego games, Paul was able to dance through the disagreements with more ease and grace.

I am not saying that taking a stand is unhealthy or wrong. It's actually natural and engaging to take a stand or to have an opinion. But it becomes a problem when you become positional, when you are not open to hearing or learning about other ways, thoughts or beliefs. You stop learning when you become positional and declare that your way is the right way and all other ways are no good. This is what causes wars, why there are suicide bombers, why there are mass shootings in sacred spaces, because these people have become so positional they believe that their way is the only way and therefore all others should die because they don't believe the same.

There is an old Buddhist saying, "You must be flexible or else you will break." Imagine your body bending back and forth, back and forth, and if you are not able to stay flexible and open, you will break. Your mind will also break. When the mind breaks, you become crazy and do heinous things like open fire in a mosque. This is the ultimate ego at play.

This is not to say that your father, who was born in another generation, will understand these teachings. It's okay if he doesn't and don't waste your time trying to make him. You don't want to cause even more conflict trying to get another person to "understand" these teachings. But what can shift for you is to see these games in action, even with another who knows nothing about these games. When you are able to see, "Oh, there is dad's ego being positional," you no longer have the drive or fight inside of you to "be right." You instead are able to soften and to allow, knowing that it's not worth it to be right and make him wrong. Just see the ego in action and let go.

Journal:

1. Think of a relationship where you play these six ego games the most.

2. How are the ego games affecting this relationship? What are they causing?

3. Is the relationship important enough for you to start becoming aware of these six games the ego plays and are you able to *see* the games in action? Can you catch yourself in the act of playing these ego games and take a pause before responding?

4. How have these ego games kept you holding on to your story of trauma and/or PTSD?

5. Are you ready and able to let go and can you for-give?

Ego Eradicator: A Kundalini Yoga Practice

If you want to start a daily practice that will help keep your ego in check, go to my YouTube channel (https://www.youtube.com/watch?v=kuOM4VUejfs) where I have a short video on how to practice Ego Eradicator or read below.

Ego Eradicator (one minute to three minutes)

1. Sit in easy pose (simple cross-legged posture) or sit in a chair with both feet on the ground.

2. Raise the arms to a sixty-degree angle. Curl the fingertips onto the pads at the base of the fingers. Plug the thumbs into the sky.

3. Eyes closed, concentrate above the head, and do Breath of Fire. Breath of Fire is rapid breathing done in and out through the nose. The emphasis is on the exhalation and the in-halation will automatically happen. Think of blowing out a candle with your nose. If you ever feel light headed, go to long deep breath-ing and once you feel balanced, pick up the Breath of Fire again.

To End

1. Inhale and touch the thumb-tips together over-head.

2. Exhale and apply mulbandh (root lock). Tightening all of the sex organs, anus, pulling all of the energy in the pelvic floor up.

3. Inhale and relax.

This exercise opens the lungs, brings the hemispheres of the brain to a state of alertness, and consolidates the magnetic field.

CHAPTER 10
COMMIT. SHOW UP.

Step 6: Elevate

You've made it this far and I am so proud of you! I trust that you're beginning to feel safe again, back "inside" your body, and that an inner shift has begun to occur for you. I trust that an opening has started to form, and this opening is allowing for a more natural, organic way to heal, grow, and transform.

Remember, I am not a doctor. I am not advising you to stop taking your pills, scripts, booze, or meds. Ultimately, you have the freedom to choose and do with your life what you want. You have free will. But I want you to listen to those words again and to listen to them carefully; *you have the freedom and the power to do with your life what you choose to do. You have free will.* No one has that power over you unless you give it to him or her. No one has power over your body-mind-spirit unless you give it to him or her. Take back control of your body, your mind, and your spirit and say, "This is who I want to be in the world, and this is how I want to show up!"

I Am Practice

You can order an "I AM" deck on my website catherine-scherwenka.com, but it is not necessary in order to do this practice.

Find a comfortable seat either on the floor or in a chair. Have your palms face up and hands relaxed on your thighs. As yourself, "Do I believe I have the power to choose for myself? What am I choosing for me today?"

And then fill in the blank: I am (courage, wise, beautiful, strong, unique, blessed, grateful…).

Close your eyes, inhaling deeply, and as you inhale, feel any fear, anxiety, insecurity, doubt, worry, or unease in the body. As you exhale, say the, "I AM" statement you chose. Continue this for seven long, deep breaths. On the last inhalation, hold the breath for a count of seven and see your entire body, cells, bones, and beyond filled with the essence of your "I am…" statement.

See it. Feel it. Be it!

Lastly, place both of your hands on the center of your chest, which is the heart center, and as you continue the long deep breathing, feel both your hands rise and fall with each breath. As you do this for seven more breaths, feel gratitude for your body, for your breath, for your mind, your brain, and for life. As this is happening, put a gentle smile on your face, even if you don't want to do this, try it and see what might shift.

Release the breath and throughout your day, remember your "I am…" commitment!

My Mojo

I've shared with you what has worked for me. The reason I am so deeply passionate about this work is because of the depth and expansion of healing that has occurred for me from doing this inner work and the opportunities that arose from that.

We spend so much of our lives focused on outer fitness and strength, so why don't we spend as much time – if not more – on the inner fitness and strength? You must remember that you are building new muscles in the brain; you are redirecting those neural pathways from stress and anxiety to something more positive, productive, and beneficial. By forming these new neural pathways, you are able to go from feeling separate and disconnected, to feeling radiant and connected, from feeling lacking and empty to feeling abundant and full, from feeling shame and guilt to feeling empowered and courageous.

But it is up to you to do the work. The inner work.

And this type of work requires commitment, dedication, and consistency. One of the many things I have found from working with so many clients from all different walks of life is that they don't generally have a problem being committed, dedicated, and consistent to certain parts of their lives or for other people, places, or things, but when it comes to being committed, dedicated, and consistent to their inner world and to their own growth and transformation? This is difficult.

Maybe you are one of those people who says, "I'm going to start my daily practice of yoga and meditation tomorrow, and I'll also stop eating carbs and sugar."

You do it for four days, and you feel great; you start seeing results, but then your friend invites you to a house-warming party one night, and you end up staying later than you intended. That little inner voice inside you keeps saying, "I'm only going to have a little nibble of this bread with cheese and then I'll go back on the no carb diet tomorrow." But then days pass and then weeks and you've officially fallen off the wagon of health and vitality again and back onto the path of not taking care of yourself and not feeling great both in the body and also in the mind.

Not only does your body not appreciate or like this, but the mind has a heyday when you "fail," berating yourself for being weak, for not being able to stick to it, for always giving in, and the cycle continues on.

This happened to me a lot, and it was one of the most frustrating parts from when I wasn't living in health, vitality, and alignment with my true wishes and desires for myself. It was as if I was constantly going against the grain, against myself that was creating a war within.

Can You Relate?

It was from this awareness that I became inspired to create personal one-on-one sessions, workshops, and courses both in person and online, that not only facilitate a sort of kick-start to get someone back on track but also hold him or her accountable when the mind starts to creep in with its cunning and conniving ways to derail you.

Sometimes you need outside support in order to grow. You need to be held accountable. You need the support and encouragement of others. You need to know you are not the only one going through whatever it is you are going through and that whatever you are going through is okay. You need the external reflections from others to see, feel, and experience that you are okay, that you might slip and fall sometimes, but that someone will be there to help get you back on track reminding you that we are all connected, that we all have very similar experiences, and that ultimately, we are all one.

Am I Worth It?

During one of multiple-month online immersion courses I was facilitating, I had a mother of two very active young boys who also happened to be an attorney working full time who felt there was no way she could take one hour a week in order to be on the video call for the group session let alone commit to a daily morning practice of twenty minutes. We spent some one-on-one time and explored where this limiting belief was coming from.

A-ha, it ended up being one of the most common limiting beliefs that run through the collective consciousness: that she didn't deserve it. She ended up committing to the multi-month program and by the end of the course, she said she felt like she had not only created a new body (which she felt had been ruined after birthing two healthy, strong boys), but also had built this new relationship with her mind that she never knew could exist.

Instead of being made use of by the mind, she felt she had become more of the observer where she could see the mind in action, therefore not reacting to it as much as being able to respond.

This was reflected out into her relationships that then allowed for deeper meaning, connection, and love with those she was closest to. She also rekindled her relationship to her higher sacred self, which she had shut down as a child, growing up in Catholicism, a faith she never felt like she belonged in.

Sometimes what you need is to do it, to commit – commit to yourself, to your practice, to your health, to whatever it is that you are wanting and desiring for your body-mind-spirit in order to feel more radiant, alive, healthy, and vibrant.

Remember, it comes from the inside out. The radiance shines from inside.

What is happening in your external world is a reflection of what is happening inside of you.

One of the most predictable games the mind will play at this point is to tell you "I don't have the money" or "I don't have the time." This is the oldest trick of the mind, yet probably the most effective ones that keep you from committing and saying yes. The mind doesn't want to change; it doesn't want you to cultivate awareness. The mind knows that the more awareness you cultivate, the greater the ability to "see" as if pointing a flashlight on the thinking, and once you start seeing the thinking process and how it all plays and acts on each other. It's like catching a thief in the act of stealing, it'll drop whatever it has taken and run. The same holds true for the mind. As soon as you "see" the shenanigans that it's up to, it'll drop whatever or wherever it's got a hold on you and disappear. This is when we drop into that place of deep inner peace that we are all striving for, but the reality is, there is nowhere to go because what we search for outside ourselves is right there inside of you! It is you!

When we are able to let go of resisting what is happening inside and around us and instead stop to feel, be aware, be connected, let go, forgive, and elevate, that is when our internal world changes and we can truly be the change we want to see in the world.

Don't try to rearrange the external furniture in an attempt to try to make your internal world feel better. Instead go in, feel what is there, allow for what is there, connect, let go, forgive, elevate. This is the path to the newly upgraded Jedi version of yourself. Trust me. I've done it. I've seen it. I am it!

CHAPTER 11
YOU ARE THE TEACHER AND THE TEACHING IS YOURSELF

We have come to the conclusion of this journey – this journey that took you from feeling chaotic and frustrated to feeling more stable and grounded. I hope by now it feels as if our bond has grown and that because you know more of where I've come from and my own experience with PTSD, trauma, and stress, as well as helping others with theirs we can drop in more deeply and continue together on this path of growth and transformation.

You should have a pulse as to where you are inside the spectrum of trauma and where you spend most of your time, looking at the scale from zero to one hundred, reminding yourself that it's okay, no matter where you are at; you just have to become aware and move from that place, not from where you think you should be. When you wake up in the morning, you might be around zero if you're lucky, but probably more around twenty for most of us and by midmorning, depending on your stress level, you could easily pop up to eighty or ninety without even being aware of it. Start monitoring where you are at and have the intention of bringing yourself back down to the neutral zone as often as you can. At least get below fifty.

You now have a vision for where you'd like to be in six months, in one year, and in five years, and it all begins by stopping, taking a pause, and using the physical body to let you know where you are holding on to the trauma and the stress. The body doesn't lie and will always speak to you if you listen.

You've learned the importance of becoming aware of the internal discomfort, how to lean into it instead of running away from it, and what your escape mechanism is when you're attempting to avoid and not go inward. Is it drinking, smoking, shopping, or social media? Or is it something else? Not judging any of it, just observing and becoming aware of what your vice of choice is and instead of going for that – lean in.

You learned why it is important to feel a connection, why creating sacred space in your home would support this feeling of being connected. You experienced power-ful meditation techniques that can be used as your med-ication to help move you beyond the thinking and the mind where you will become more of the observer and the witness of the mind instead of thinking you are the mind and its thoughts. This keeps you more present, in the moment and not always stuck in the past or the fu-ture which keeps you in that fight/flight/freeze mode.

The next big piece is the letting go and the for-giveness, realizing that by holding on to the hurt, pain, and the trauma, you are only hurting yourself and not the one you blame for your trauma and/or PTSD. This can be a huge release, a huge relief, and a gift that'll keep on giving because you are making more space for grace. By doing this, you are more likely to drop into your Jedi Super Powers and admit that perhaps the next best thing to do is to continue moving forward on this journey, but with the support and reflections of others around you who are working on the same thing.

And then you elevate. You grow in consciousness, you grow in who you are and how you show up in the world, you shine your light bright and you be the change you want to see in the world.

Why This Book?

I knew for a long time I was going to write a book, but I just didn't know when or how. After 9/11, I felt I had a story to tell, something to share with the world about my experience, what it gave me, and how I chose to navigate through it. From 2013, when I left India after living there for three years, I traveled nonstop for five years, going from Bali, to Ireland, to Canada, to Mexico, and all over the United States, teaching, sharing, growing through experience, as well as continuing my education at the academy I study at in India. I'll never forget, in June 2017, telling my business partner that I was marking out of my calendar the first two weeks of November that year to do nothing. I wasn't flying anywhere, teaching anything; I was going to do nothing. I had many people contact me from June to October to invite me to come and teach, but I politely kept declining, remembering I had committed to taking off those first two weeks of November to do nothing.

Most of you will remember the October 1 shooting that took place during the Route 91 Harvest festival at Mandalay Bay in Las Vegas in 2017. To this day, it is the deadliest mass shooting in US modern-day history; it left fifty-eight people dead – fifty-nine including the shooter.

Again, another mass tragedy devastated our country, leaving so many of us reeling, asking those existential questions again like "Why?" or "What's the point?"

So many people affected on many levels – the loved ones who were lost in the tragedy, the ones who survived with injuries, the ones who survived with no injuries, the first responders who tended to the injured both physically and emotionally at the scene and thereafter, and who also very much honored and respected those killed in the incident.

Our country again was on high alert, people in shock, trauma, dealing with more trauma and PTSD.

I was on my last tour in Northern California on October 8 when I received a phone call from a dear friend whom I had known for many years from the academy we studied at in India. She was calling to see if there was any way I might be able to fly into Las Vegas to guide meditation for the Clark County Coroner's Office as she was leaving to go to India and needed someone she could count on to do the work. I was humbled, and I instantly knew the cycle had completed itself, from who I was after 9/11 to October 1 and who I had grown into. I chuckled, not at what she was asking of me, but because I had blocked those two weeks out of my calendar for six months knowing in every cell of my being that I couldn't say yes to any offers to come and teach – not knowing this was coming. I accepted the offer with great honor, and what we thought would be a temporary relief program for the first responders turned into what could potentially be the example for our country in how to deal with and heal from trauma, PTSD, hurt, and pain in alternative ways.

My Intention for You

I wrote this book in order for you to take your life back.
I wrote this book for you to feel safe in your body again.
I wrote this book for you to feel like you have a purpose in life again.

I wrote this book for you to feel inspired, encouraged, and ready to engage and create the life that you know you are meant to be living.

Trauma and PTSD can and will ruin your life if you allow it.

Remember, you have the choice to allow it to ruin your life or to take control back over your body-mind-spirit and make a shift, a change through feeling, awareness, connection, letting go, and forgiveness. You have that power and when you tap into this power, you elevate. You connect to that which is greater than you, to your higher self, and when that happens? You reclaim your magic!

I hope this book inspires you to keep going, to go deeper within, to continue peeling back the layers of "the onion" that'll continue directing to the inner core of your being where there is nothing but emptiness, nothing but bliss, nothing but pure acceptance of the what is.

The journey never ends and there is no destination.

Say yes to reclaiming your life and all its magic.

Say yes to being ready to witness all of the synchronicities that happen just from saying yes!

May your life be blessed.

May you bless all those who come into contact with you.

May you live with your head up and your heart out.

And remember, you are the only one and unique expression and version that God, Creator, Divine made of you.

Honor who that is, who you are.

Respect who you are.

And most important of all, be who you are!

ACKNOWLEDGMENTS

There are so many people, places, and things I'd like to appreciate and acknowledge with regard to this book, but first and foremost are my teachers: Sri Amma, Sri Bhagavan, Krishnaji, and Preethaji. Without your wisdom, grace, love, and support, I would not be where I am today.

My parents, I wouldn't be here without you! I exist because you had a vision and a cocreation that birthed five kids and some magic. Thank you for being my parents. I love you!

I'd also like to thank my twin sister, Elizabeth Scherwenka, for connecting me to the incredible work that we do on this planet together and for being my potent reflection! My older sister, Linda McIntyre, you are my solid rock who is always there for me no matter what.

My business partner, Kristina Muller, my creative muse, my right arm, my graphic brilliance, and bestie, you always have my back, no matter what. Gratitude to Debra Apsara for holding such sacred space for my spirit to dance, dream, write, and grow in!

My two heart-centered, gorgeous brothers, thank you for just being you. My stepmother, Kandace, you have always been an inspiration to me in so many ways. Thank you for being a strong woman in my life.

To Tim, for taking care of our mom. My sis-in-laws, thank you for your beauty, love, encouragement, and support.

And for my partner, John, you are the most extraordinary visionary I've ever met; you face fear by walking through it, you don't let anyone or anything hold back your dreams, and if anyone has ever had the opportunity to meet his daughter, they'll know exactly what I mean – she's a spitting image! Brilliance in action.

To Anna, thank you for helping me to look deeper inside myself, which always leads to more growth.

And to all of my friends across the planet, there are so many people I wish I could list here and say thank you to, because without each one of you, my life would be vastly different. You are what bring color, magic and zest to my life and you have all supported me in so many countless ways. Thank you. Thank you.

To Mother Earth, for life.

ABOUT THE AUTHOR

CATHERINE SCHERWENKA is an empowered and thriving entrepreneur, globally-revered transformational workshop facilitator and Certified Kundalini Yoga Instructor. She is an inspiring mentor for youth and has led thousands of people of all ages through life-changing shifts. After the traumatic experience of 9/11, Catherine began a courageous inner-journey of healing her own trauma and PTSD. After witnessing a lack of progress with traditional talk therapies and use of prescription meds, Catherine became a strong advocate and facilitator of alternative healing methods.

Catherine lived in India for many years studying, volunteering, and deepening her understanding of the Body. Mind. Spirit connection at O&O Academy, where she learned how to navigate PTSD holistically. Through the

Academy, Catherine became a Certified Oneness Trainer, Meditator, and Transformer. She's also the founder of Inner Peace Initiative, FLY Retreats (Feel Like Yourself) and of Inner Peace for the Children. She attended both New York University and the University of Montana.

Most recently, Catherine has been pioneering a recovery wellness program for the government agencies affected by the October 1 incident in Las Vegas, Nevada, where she now resides. It is in Catherine's highest vision to see the program as a beta and become a liberation system for the entire United States.

Her passion is to help people experiencing anxious, disconnected states of being in making shifts into living more joyful, connected lives. She incorporates a wide variety of world-renown modalities including wisdom teachings, yoga, meditation, spiritual guidance, and mentoring to help people live happier, authentic, fulfilling lives.

ABOUT DIFFERENCE PRESS

Difference Press is the exclusive publishing arm of The Author Incubator, an educational company for entrepreneurs – including life coaches, healers, consultants, and community leaders – looking for a comprehensive solution to get their books written, published, and promoted. Its founder, Dr. Angela Lauria, has been bringing to life the literary ventures of hundreds of authors-in-transformation since 1994.

A boutique-style self-publishing service for clients of The Author Incubator, Difference Press boasts a fair and easy-to-understand profit structure, low-priced author copies, and author-friendly contract terms. Most importantly, all of our #incubatedauthors maintain ownership of their copyright at all times.

Let's Start a Movement with Your Message

In a market where hundreds of thousands of books are published every year and are never heard from again,

The Author Incubator is different. Not only do all Difference Press books reach Amazon bestseller status, but all of our authors are actively changing lives and making a difference.

Since launching in 2013, we've served over 500 authors who came to us with an idea for a book and were able to write it and get it self-published in less than 6 months. In addition, more than 100 of those books were picked up by traditional publishers and are now available in book stores. We do this by selecting the highest quality and highest potential applicants for our future programs.

Our program doesn't only teach you how to write a book – our team of coaches, developmental editors, copy editors, art directors, and marketing experts incubate you from having a book idea to being a published, bestselling author, ensuring that the book you create can actually make a difference in the world. Then we give you the training you need to use your book to make the difference in the world, or to create a business out of serving your readers.

Are You Ready to Make a Difference?

You've seen other people make a difference with a book. Now it's your turn. If you are ready to stop watching and start taking massive action, go to http://theauthorincubator.com/apply

"Yes, I'm ready!"

OTHER BOOKS
BY DIFFERENCE PRESS

Reverse Button™: Learn What the Doctors Aren't Telling You, Avoid Back Surgery, and Get Your Full Life Back by Abby Beauchamp

Never Too Late for Love: The Successful Woman's Guide to Online Dating in the Second Half of Life by Joan Bragar, EdD

Stronger Together: My MS Story by Chloe Cohen

Yogini's Dilemma: To Be, or Not to Be, a Yoga Teacher? by Nicole A. Grant

Come Alive: Find Your Passion, Change Your Life, Change the World! by Jodi Hadsell

Meant For More: Stop Secretly Struggling and Become a Force to Be Reckoned With by Mia Hewett

Lord, Please Save My Marriage: A Christian Woman's Guide to Thrive, Despite Her Husband's Drunken Rants by Christine Lennard

If I'm so Zen, Why Is My Hair Falling Out?: How Past Trauma and Anxiety Manifest in the Physical Body by Amanda Lera

Heal Your Trauma, Heal Your Marriage: 7 Steps to Root, Rebound, and Rise by Dr. Cheri L. McDonald

WELCOME to the Next Level: 3 Secrets to Become Unstuck, Take Action, and Rise Higher in Your Career by Sonya L. Sigler

Embrace Your Psychic Gifts: The Guide to Spiritual Awakening by Deborah Sudarsky

Leverage: The Guide to End Your Binge Eating by Linda Vang

Under the Sleeve: Find Help for Your Child Who Is Cutting by Dr. Stacey Winters

THANK YOU

Thank you for reading my book, *PTSD and a Drug-Free Me*. If you made it to the end of this book, I know that you are truly committed to healing from the hard truth that trauma and PTSD have the potential to leave a long lasting imprint on your life, but that you can heal without having to depend on alcohol, drugs, or prescription meds.

As an added bonus and an expression of my appreciation, I've created an audio-book which takes you through a deeper journey of the 6-Step STABLE process that I shared with you in the book.

If you'd like a copy of the free audio, please email **info@catherinescherwenka.com** and in the subject line, type "STABLE," and a copy of the class will be sent to you.

I would love to be a part of your support system, so please do stay in touch!

You can do so either by email (**info@catherine-scherwenka.com**), or you can find me on social media on Facebook (**https://www.facebook.com/catscherwenka/**), Instagram (@catherine_scherwenka), or on Twitter (@catscherwenka).

Many blessings to you to live a happy, healthy, fulfilling life without having the affects of trauma and PTSD holding you back!